The Tantric Hindu Bible

This is a collection of essays, letters, philosophy, and spiritual doctrines!

ISBN: 978-1-943287-01-7

Kali Manifest

I draw upon and summon the dark force of Kali, Mother Vampress! We are one being from which I draw strength and power from her blood, the Life Force of Creation. Goddess Kali, is life, death, and the undead! We are the eternal spirit and eternal body. I shall reincarnate eternally! I am immortal through your power oh great Dark Mother Kali!

The Future of Human Civilization Part 1-2

Part 1

Question: In this spiritually advanced society you speak of, how does one advance in status? Is it completely anti-capitalist, pro-communist or man returning to nature?

Answer: It's a little bit of each, but definitely a theocracy as opposed to the current semi-secular forms of government which force their religious moral-values through majority rule anyway. It would also be in contrast to a technocracy with science being the substitute for religion. The last thing on earth we need is to be ruled by scientists who have no spirituality or spiritual development and have a goal to have us rely upon machines instead of our natural traditional work-service skills. First the rich class and their corporations try to strip us of our skills to control us through wages in their factories and then comes technocratic scientists doing the same thing except that it's one big state corporation we are forced to rely upon and become enslaved by. If we have no independent specialized skills we not only become dependents of machines we lose our natural survival skills so if and when the machines do cease to function we won't have any knowledge of how to survive without them. This kind of fear would keep us dependent upon them even more. This is not about being against science or machines, it's about being dependent upon them and allowing them to control our future. I believe we already are too dependent upon machines and that science and technology is being used in a very negative way to benefit the capitalists. Also, I believe that getting back to nature is more advanced than relying upon machines or chemicals for every solution. Buddhists are some of the most spiritually advanced people and they lived in caves for hundreds of years. This has no negative relation to their highly evolved state and only shows even more how advanced they are. They make use of the natural environment which is far healthier than modern industrialized homes and costs little to nothing but their own labor to fix up or even carve out. The future of science should also be looking inward and back to nature as a path of progress. The limitations of capitalism are created by the capitalists and the rich class themselves by refusing to give up their wealth and status. As for traditional skills, what is wrong with hand looming, farming, massage, craft making, etc.? This is advancement, not having everything created by machines. While still in a capitalist system, this helps to free us from exploitation from large corporations as we work for communities and ourselves. When capitalism collapses and the monetary system erodes away then these skills are what will keep civilization moving along. We will be neither dependent completely upon private or state corporations nor will we be dependent completely upon machines.

Part 2

Why do we need to advance in status at all? The current foundation of the capitalist economic system is based upon profit. A truly advanced civilization should be based solely upon helping the people 100% and never profit. I have envisioned a cross over system that can be used while the capitalist system still exists and therefore our system will co-exist until the time when the capitalist system implodes from the final lack of confidence in the capitalist system or its stock markets, class submersion, and mass conversion away from capitalism in general.

This cross over system will make use of credits in two forms, one kind that are spendable and a second kind that goes toward your class level. This means we create a systemized ascending class order which is easily and realistically scalable within a few years. The highest level would be equivalent of that of a millionaire today. This is a semi-egalitarian system which gives equal benefits per level and yet increasing the amount of benefits per higher level. I have proposed a 9 level system, but that can be reduced to simplify if necessary. Citizens can earn credits on top of their monthly benefits, simply because they wish to out of boredom, for fun, for extra incentives. The credits will serve to purchase crafts and services which would allow them to exceed their monthly benefits. Free guilds would teach them craft and service skills. And others may charge credits for their training, etc. There will be a 9 million credit cap for credit earnings.

All major resources and technology will be owned by the people collectively and will be free to use according to their benefit level. Certain restrictions and bans will be on specific technologies which are deemed dangerous to the people and civilization. This refers to weapons technologies which will be highly controlled in our weapon free civilization. There will be two kinds of citizen members during the cross over period. The first kind is the Internal Member and the second kind is the External Member. Internal Members will live within the Temples and not use any external form of monetary unit. External Members will live the way most people do now and simply contribute to the Temple now and then.

Once the capitalist system completely collapses then External Members will begin to start moving into the Temples and become Internal Members because there will be nothing left for them to turn to and those that want to stay in their homes may do so. From this system you will see that no one goes without. All are automatically entered into class level one with required benefits. Internal Members experience the true and full form of the egalitarian system because they chose to give up everything material from the beginning. They do not make use of credits, have full class status, etc., but they can use credits if they wish. Internal Members have to obviously do their work though or like anyone else will be removed if they do not work for at least one year.

Everyone needs a living shelter, clothing, food, bathing and toilet facilities, and training. These are all provided for free at a high quality standard level. Everyone is then obligated to work for at least one year on their chosen craft or service. This is a service to your community and you are rewarded for this with an honorable credit and class elevation.

The honorable credit determines your class status and can never be taken away. A citizen may now end their work career if they wish and simply live on their monthly benefits because they have fulfilled their service to their people.

Though most people will grow bored and wish to do something and seek more benefits. Those who sell their crafts or provide their services can do this as their mandatory year of work and others may choose to do other Temple jobs. Citizens can own smaller items and crafts. The object is not to become a large business like today's corporations, but simply to have fun and provide friendly competition at the most. Crafts allow people to provide an alternative of products to those people bored of wearing, etc. free Temple products. People who enter the actual Temple areas of worship must wear the required Temple clothing.

There is a mix of freedoms and rules that allow for room to breathe. Many other people who do not like this Temple System will seek out other Temple Systems and Scientific Systems. Many types of systems will exist for different people to turn to as the capitalist system collapses on itself. The thing to remember is that there is always something better or room for improvement. Those that tell you the capitalist system is as good as it gets are liars! And those that do not seek out better systems have failed their people, their children, and themselves with their lack of imagination and vision.

Getting In Touch With Your-Self

The idea of getting in touch with Self is the connection we make with the greater power of the Universal Creation because we are all One Great Consciousness. We have to realize that we are only smaller aspects of the whole and grand divinity of Creation. This is one of the reasons I really like the Hindu Pantheon it's so vast and reveals a myriad of different aspects of Creation that can be understood in a multitude of God and Goddess forms. These are all also reflected through us as lesser deities, yet always one with Creation. Creation not only expresses it-self in multitudinous forms but it perceives itself through us as we experience the perception through countless diversities. Basically, Creation is perceiving itself through us and many other life forms and forms of existence.

Worker Charkha or the Wheel of Workers

1. The Farmers

They grow the needed fruit, vegetables, rice, cotton, dye plants, spices, etc.

2. The Spinners

They spin the yarn needed to make the clothing, etc.

3. The Clothing Makers

They make all the clothing, etc.

4. The Food Preparers

They prepare the food, water, etc.

5. The Craft Workers

They make all the crafts, and building work.

6. The Teachers

They teach all arts, crafts, knowledge, etc.

7. The Satyagraha Army (non-violent)

They train to be non-violent soldiers to secure our rights and freedom.

8. The Priest/ess Healers

They perform all the different religious ceremonies, meditate, give spiritual advice, and perform healing arts of various kinds.

9. The Musicians and Dancers *New

They learn, practice, play, perform, and teach all forms of music and dance.

10. The Service Workers *New

They are all other types of service workers.

Caesar's Swaraj

I don't like college much. I follow the beliefs of Dr. Timothy Leary, and others who have shown us that mainstream schools just brainwash us by making us copy their facts, instead of learning ourselves. Self-learning, smaller schools, and trade schools are much better. His motto was "Turn on, tune in, and drop out." He was a professor during the hippy counter culture movement of the 60's. And if schools are free it's even better. Schools are so expensive. Most poor people can't afford them. I believe all school should be free.

I want to build my temple like a big commune society. And everyone helps out, making crafts, and providing services, etc. So, a college degree is not necessary, etc. People share the responsibility and that's very equality driven. I didn't even go to high school that long. I dropped out, though I went back for my diploma at night school later on. Most of what I know, I taught myself. I don't think it's important that people have to go to college, and I would like to see them save their money for better things, join me, or invest in my temple, where they would always have a home and a position. But if that's what they really want, to go to college, then that's ok too. But it sure doesn't help my temple and our people, unless they come join me later on.

The idea is a group of people working interdependently together will reduce the capitalist burdens the rich class puts on the poverty slave or worker class. Being totally independent in a capitalist system makes you powerless and the poor have to struggle to rise above the high costs of living on your own. When a group comes together it divides the burdens and costs. It also undermines the capitalist systems method of keeping people in poverty. So, then they can break free from that poverty.

Poverty only exists in a society that forces its monetary system upon everyone and where the rich class and middle class control all the resources. That's corruption. If people have access to their own way to produce food, water, clothing, shelter, etc., then they have successfully defeated poverty without any monetary support. And most other things they do not need in the first place. I'd rather have people drop out from school and not go to college to join me and help invest in my temple being set up like a commune. This will truly help people more than college will.

It will truly help the people because we have to start somewhere and sometime. We have to start at the bottom and we have to start now. True change for the better for the people will never come from the top down first. Change has to come from the bottom up. We have to start now and that means people have to make a sacrifice for the good of the whole community, our commune, our temple. We can no longer just think of ourselves in a selfish, greedy, mercenary fashion. This only breeds the type of people the rich class need to maintain control over their poverty slave class or the worker class. We have to be concerned about our environment, our health, our future, and our present. We have to stop conforming to a system that is destroying the world and oppressing the people. We have to begin to unite for a greater cause than ourselves. I am here to help those that will

help me on my quest for Spiritual Evolution on our path toward Divine Human Utopia, glimmering with the enchantment of Sacred Freedom and Egalitarian Self-Government.

Caesar's Ashram and Temple Commune

Caesar's Ashram Project is designed to raise money for our Temple Ashram. We accept donations, your volunteer services, your support, and membership. Caesar's Ashram is the core of our Temple foundation. It will provide healing and spiritual services to both our members and those outside our community that wish to pay for our services and projects. You may have seen the Workers Charkha, which our Temple Ashram will be based upon. This is a microcosm within the macrocosm of the world community which may participate in our Worker Charkha. Meaning that outside members that follow the pattern of our Worker Charkha can trade with our main Temple of Kama Ashram, and other Temples, Ashrams, Communes, etc. Those that join our Temple Ashram will devote their energies and time toward developing and expanding our Ashram in the name of our Creation Consciousness. We are here to help our people find unity with Creation, to heal them, and to develop proper living values and environment according to our unique Dharma. This means that those who join our Temple Ashram do so not for personal benefit besides true freedom, securing our rights, Swaraj, improved health, well-being, self-perfection, and peace of mind. Those that seek to profit can reside outside of our Ashram becoming part of the larger World Ashram, and may trade with our community, etc. Contact me if you are interested in joining and helping out with my Ashram.

The Two Main Types of Women

There are two main types of Women. The first is the type that wants a controlled relationship with current judeo-christian mainstream or orthodox rules. The second is the type that wants to raise power in the form of money, sexual energy, etc. Then there are many variations on these types that are all sub-types. We focus on the main two types. The first type we can call the Anti-Whore. The second type is the Whore and the Holy Whore. We must define the difference between the Whore and the Holy Whore. The basic Whore is mercenary and self-fulfilling. The Holy Whore serves her or his people fulfilling their desires in service to the People, the Temple, and the Deities. The basic Whore always charges something for their sexual favors. The Holy Whore may charge sometimes or just to those who are not Temple Members and otherwise provides virtually free service provided the Members do their part in the Temple Society. The goal of our Temple is to teach and spread the values of the Holy Whore among our people and potential members. The Anti-Whore does not serve the needs of our people or Temple and so we work to eliminate this mentality from our society.

Behind The God

Behind the God Shiva is the Goddess Kali-Shakti or Yellamma! The first energy of the universe is the feminine spiritual energy that divides into two becoming masculine material and feminine spiritual energies that unite in a cosmic dance and sexual union which brings forth the material Creation. So, from the one comes the two and from the two comes the many and return to the one. The one deity becomes two and then one perpetually in mystical union or the divine marriage. This is the Androgynous God/Goddess.

We worship the main deity Kali through devotion, ritual pujas or offerings, ritual dancing, musical arts, sexual healing/fulfillment, ritual tantra, by becoming Devadasi Priestesses and Priests, vegetarian/pescetarian feasting, massage healing, yoga healing, Ayurveda healing, martial arts, magick arts, helping to end the suffering of others, and self-sacrifice for the good of the whole, etc. We also worship the many other deities of the Hindu pantheon which are all aspects of the non-dual and dual Creation. In its dual form we mainly worship Kali-Shakti and Shiva. Another pair that can be focused upon is Radha and Krishna as well as many other deities.

The New Born Devadasi

Devadasi Temple Dancers probably originated from the Goddess Kali-Yellamma and Shiva branch of Shakti Hinduism. It was practiced for over 1000 years in the Karnataka region of South India. The modern opponents of the Kali-Yellamma branch call them a cult to demonize them and their beliefs. The Devadasi were established in many regions under many deities. The Chola Empire established the Devadasi system probably into a far more organized system in many temples including a main complex of the Brihadeesvarar temple, Thanjavur, India under the main god Shiva among others. The Brahmins established the Devadasi as a caste like they do all other forms of craft and service workers. Each caste has its privileges, benefits, and recognitions. The Mahari Devadasi of Orissa established the Devadasi system in the Jagannath temple complex under the main deity of Lord Jagannath a form of Krishna and incarnation of Vishnu. They also worshipped many Goddess deities. This was the only region where the Devadasi were celibate at least supposed to be. All other regions practiced and promoted prostitution or promiscuity outside of marriage but at the same time caste values were probably expected to be followed for those of higher castes especially women. This depended upon the region and caste values that were established and popular. The Devadasi were immune since they were married to the God or Goddess or both as one Androgynous deity. They were considered respectable on the level of a Priest and had such authority and freedom. If we read in the Kama Sutra we will see how ancient courtesans were well educated and trained in the arts. They had great freedom and liberal lifestyles. They were honored, respected, and glorified. This is the proper way to address a Devadasi of either promiscuous or celibate path. There were both men and women Devadasi.

The division between the opposing value systems has continued to this day. The Yellamma Branch still promotes the beauty of fulfilling the desires of men and women as devotion to the deities of Yellamma and Shiva. Yellamma is an incarnation of Kali. They advocate free love, promiscuity, and prostitution, etc. The opposing majority of the modern branches of the Vaishnavites and Shaivites condemn such practices as immoral banning these practices by law. This has been backed by international right-wing groups spearheaded by feminist christians that work to ban prostitution world-wide! As supporters of prostitution, promiscuity, etc., and believers in the forces of Creation especially the underlying feminine Goddess Power it is our duty to give support to the Kali-Yellamma Branch and the full resurrection of the Devadasi System! This is our foundation for the new age Kali Temple where we will teach the arts of traditional Indian dance with the full erotic aspects restored, teach the arts of music including instruments, singing, etc., and the arts of the Courtesan with full respect, dignity, and honor restored! So, our Devadasi will be married to the temple and may marry others, be celibate, promiscuous, prostitute themselves, trade, be educated, etc. We support the rights of our people and the Devadasi! We support freedom and devotion to the temple! These are choices that we give to our people and do not take away their rights. Glory to the Yellamma Order and glory to the new born Devadasi!

Tantric Hinduism, Devadasism, Tantracism

Tantric Hinduism embraces various practices and deities like Shiva, Kali, etc., Temple Worship, Devadasi Priest/ess, Tantric Priest/ess, Classical Indian Dance, Classical Indian Music, Escorting, Sexual Healing, Massage Healing, Yoga, Meditation, Magick, etc. This is a religion combining many aspects of Spirituality, Devadasism, Tantricism, etc.

My Thoughts on the Zeitgeist Movement Part 1

I was reading on that site Zeitgeist Movement. I have very similar beliefs but I wrap mine in my religion and I only concentrate on my own Temple and People. I see some major flaws in that guys system which will cause it to fail. They are things that I thought through already and which caused me to develop my beliefs and goals in such a way. For example he talks about a centralized system for the entire world. The first thing about that idea is that it's impossible with the variety of cultures and beliefs that exist which has been an ongoing problem and always will be one. That is why I believe a collective of different groups, beliefs, etc. that are remotely similar would be more realistic and they have organizations like that now.

Another problem would be that of security. You cannot maintain something of that magnitude without a security force and so it tells me that there is a secret police system in that guys agenda somewhere because he must realize that people simply by human nature will not cooperate no matter how much education and mental brainwashing they put into them. And my solution to that obviously would be each group has their own security to maintain their personal stability. We see this already in the different organizations that exist.

Another problem is that the existing organizations are not simply going to go away or crumble so easily, they change and mutate and force their citizens to change to maintain the same level of benefits, authority, etc. So, they will do everything in their power to stop any group from taking that away from them. So, you are talking about a long slow process of change and adaptation that both sides will have to endure and work to prove their worth and overall greater benefit to the people in general while living and working under the laws and forces of the ruling authority. This could still take hundreds of years despite the reality of their corruption, enslavement, and exploitation of the people.

He tried to say it was not a Utopian based system and yet it is one. He also tried to disassociate his system from Socialism or Communism and yet his system has many of the major principles of those systems. And they have been working for hundreds of years now to establish a good working system under those principles. They have worked and they have failed. Trial and error will eventually create the perfect working model. I do call my system a form of New Age Socialism or New Age Communism. You might as well call it something similar to what it is similar to in principles rather than try to deny it or disassociate from it altogether.

His propaganda comparisons to his system and the current one is pretty good and much like my own. The other thing I wanted to point out was once you eliminate the money there is a vacuum left behind where people will still want to naturally have more and of course they will want more incentives. Humans will always be natural beings that will naturally want more. Though we can set limitations, but we must give room so that people will feel dignified and fulfilled in that regard. So, I created a systemized (I hate the word systematized) Class System with Credits. Though humans will have all essential needs provided, they can also earn credits for services and crafts to buy or exchange even

more benefits. Also, allowing direct barter or trade of products is essential too. I can talk about more of my system later which has far more detail and structure.

The purpose of civilization is to help the people 100% and that is what it must be based upon and not solely upon profit as it is in this capitalist system. Original barter was a good system, but then people wanted to control everything more, take a cut of the goods traded, and have a more universal tool and it became known as the base standard wealth of civilization and in modern times money. So, now kings can tax their citizens and control the wealth and power of their kingdoms. They used all different forms for the base standard from salt to gold and despite what that guy says it's always been a resource based economic system. And they used one main resource to value their other wealth and then paper money. This has been gold in many systems.

Once they removed gold from the u.s. standard what did it turn to? I mean could be oil? Though they still print up money whenever they need it and inflation goes higher and higher! In my opinion the capitalist system doesn't function correctly without the rich class constantly bringing in new sources of wealth to feed their system. Meaning that they would need to keep conquering smaller countries, suck out their resources, and exploit their people in order to maintain their wealth and power. If they don't then class submergence would occur. The entire capitalist system will come crumbling down when their main resources upon which they base their wealth become scarce or are unattainable.

They used to carry out many of their wars more covertly and now more and more overtly because they have no other choice. And so for the next few hundred years you'll see more and more bullying type wars overtly to capture more resources like oil from iraq, etc. It will be a horrible economy unless they work harder to switch their system over to other fuels they can control and are not as scarce. Then they will have more stability for a time. They always seem to adapt, so this guy with his zeitgeist movement is only knowingly developing a system which will not be universal and only benefit his group of followers and we won't see the end of the capitalist system overnight as the Socialists and Communists told us over hundred years ago.

My Thoughts on the Zeitgeist Movement Part 2

There is another point I failed to mention and that is you can't truly separate church and state, it can never be done. This is because all people will adopt a specific moral-value system which generally exists already, in the past, or a re-created one like my own. And believe it or not a majority of atheists cling to the judeo-christian moral-value system which is the core of the christian church. There will also never be a world with a majority of atheists! To me science is just another religion, there is no exact truth. For them to claim it to be is just another religious dogma. The same is true for scientology and psychology, etc. And this zeitgeist group will have a core moral-value system as well!

If it is exactly the same as the judeo-christian one, then in my book they are allies of the judeo-christians! This would make them basically the enemies of my temple. Some talk about them not having a bias toward one belief or another, but in my opinion that is impossible when you break it down to this level. I'm also using a science or a religious science that I developed in my temple which I find helps break down things even more. This science is called The Science of Animal Dominion. And it focuses more directly on humans. There are 4 major laws of this science. (1. Dominate or be dominated. 2. Strength in numbers. 3. New and better knowledge prevails over old and useless knowledge. 4. Order controls chaos.)

According to this system humans are perpetually locked in a battle with themselves and everything else for dominion until we cease to exist. Science does not elevate us from this primeval programming. It only makes us more dangerous and as one order weakens and collapses another will rise to take its place. That guy who started that movement knows that it won't ever realistically come into being without a security force, a political system, and obviously using the current monetary systems. And what I was saying is that it's always been a resource based system. They have to have something to value money against.

The problem is they have been undermining their own system by printing money up whenever they need it. I think capitalism with their type of class system was built by corrupt rich class people in the first place and therefore designed to maintain a perpetual poverty slave class. So, it's a horrible system in the first place which is doomed to fail over and over as they keep trying to fix it. Ironically, they always use Socialist methods to fix it or temporarily patch it together until the next big crisis.

In order for his movement to work, first they would need mass propaganda and recruiting to gain mass numbers into their religious cult. And the fact is it's just another religion and cult like my organization. I simply believe that I have a far better system. I think it would be horrible to allow scientists to control everything. People seem to forget that scientists are making all those chemicals in everything we eat that is making us sick and other chemicals that destroy the environment. They make weapons and nuclear bombs. They have no spiritual center! They work for profit just like the rest of the mercenary scum.

Some scientists may have a spiritual center, but most do not. Atheists are the worst people to be in control of anything, because most lack that spiritual center. Ultimately, I think this guy is just giving people a spin fantasy for their money and living the good life. I have not seen any real solutions in his flawed system that can realistically work. I have worked out the same flaws in my system which is far more advanced. In the future we may even become rivals based upon the science I was telling you about even if we have many of the same goals. I ultimately do not want to live in a technocracy ruled by scientists and engineers. They will have us all depending upon machines and I think we should be returning to nature to advance. So, I definitely support my kind of theocracy.

Modern Feminists

I support an egalitarian and equality driven society but today's conservative feminists champion christian moral dogmas, laws, and are brutally cruel toward men, as well as traditional roles for Women which are not exactly spiritually wrong. Today's Women rightly have a choice of career and of motherhood, but what is wrong with trying to put an importance upon traditional roles of pleasing a man and having children? I would say nothing at all! In Annie Besant's time her activism is justified because of the extreme inequality that existed and the limitations placed upon Women. More liberal minded feminists today are more naturally allied with my beliefs and goals.

Satanic Kali Temple of Kama Intro

Welcome to our Temple of Kama or Sacred Love-Sex! Our goal is to bring mystical enlightenment through Divine Sexuality. We believe that we can end all suffering through Sexual Shakti Goddess Power or Serpent Power. This is also known as Kundalini! We draw on the Kama Sutra, many Tantric Books, using both Vedic and Tantric Scriptures to develop a sense of Spirituality and Enlightenment. At the center of our doctrine is the mystical force 999. This is one of the main focuses in our Sexual Tantric Rituals through which we teach and achieve the Gnosis or a state of Super Conscious Enlightenment. We embrace the flesh and sexuality as divine, beautiful, and necessary for humans to be healthy both physically and mentally. The Tantric Priest and Tantric Priestess learns and teaches spiritual aspects to the students along with physical Yogic Asanas of an intimate and erotic nature.

We are a Nature Sex Cult to put it in simple words. The term Cult is interchangeable with Sect, Branch, Denomination, etc. It has been stereotyped though by groups who oppose other newer groups that have radical or even harmful beliefs and goals. This would of course be seen through different eyes and moral-value systems. Here our Tantric Hinduism or Tantracism is based upon a somewhat New Age concept of a war between opposing Moral-Value Systems rather than a war between good and evil where the people falsely believe or are taught only one true Moral-Value System exists while a ruling, dominant, or mainstream authority claims to hold that one true Moral-Value System and condemning all other beliefs as being immoral or amoral. This is this an oppressive foundation which they use to implement civil laws that strip away the rights of millions of people, especially sexual rights.

We see this concept of a war of opposing Moral-Values, and our New or Semi-New Moral-Value System that naturally opposes most right-wing values especially concerning sexuality as a radical new path to Enlightenment. Through this New Age Enlightenment we believe we can bring freedom from the oppressive right-wing forces. If you are interested in becoming a Tantric Priest, or Tantric Priestess in our new Temple contact us.

Our Temple wishes to bring natural healing arts to our people and Non-Members. Members can have free basic services but more specialized treatment will cost Members based upon how individual Healers wish to charge. Non-Members will pay for all services. Please check out our list of new healing arts that we plan to be performing or teaching, along with our India Shop. Also, I am looking for Indian Models for this site. Models will model Indian Clothing, Jewelry, etc. If you are an Indian Dancer, Devadasi, Ayurvedic Healer, Massage Healer, Yoga Teacher, Tantric Priestess, or Tantric Priest, etc. you can become a Member and list your services with your web address and email.

Tantric Hinduism Devadasism

Tantric Hinduism embraces various practices and deities like Shiva, Kali, etc., Temple Worship, Devadasi Priest/ess, Tantric Priest/ess, Classical Indian Dance, Classical Indian Music, Escorting, Sexual Healing, Massage Healing, Yoga, Meditation, Magick, etc. This is a religion combining many aspects of Spirituality, Devadasism, Tantricism, etc.

Modern Tantric Hinduism

Tantricism is a name associated with several ancient branches of Hinduism, Buddhism, etc. I've been developing a modern version which I also call Tantric Hinduism. This is a very liberal polytheistic system in opposition to other traditional conservative forms of Hinduism, etc.

Anti-Individualist Mentality

I don't agree with the individualist capitalist mentality. That's what causes the oppression of poverty and puts us into poverty slavery to begin with. We don't need grocery stores. It's time we put these corporations out of business. I strongly believe in interdependence and communal living, but of course you have to have the right kind of people to live with and work together. I am surrounded by a bunch of self-centered individualist minded spiritually backward people. They are fucking republican scum, far worse than democratic scum! The only way to get ahead and defeat these scumbag capitalists and their poverty slavery is through interdependence and working together, living together, boycotting corporations, etc.

The Mexicans as much as I dislike them (catholic, christian, and racist ones) for their racist mentality while living here and only hiring their own people as they control the temporary agencies, they intelligently use socialist methods to get ahead by bringing 20 plus family and friends into their homes to live, carpooling, bicycles, etc. The jews as much as I dislike them too, do the same thing with their religious beliefs and families all working interdependently as they help each other get ahead and their temples pay for their educations, housing, etc. and they later pay this money back. They also control the banks so they have even more power over their lives. This is powerful interdependent socialist methods internally and externally uses capitalism with their businesses profiting as much as they can. It's a win win situation for them because of their interdependence.

As for white people we are being taught to be completely independent and self-sufficient. Now, a degree of self-sufficiency isn't that bad but being totally independent makes us all economic enemies or opponents all battling each other or competing with each other to survive. This struggle is what sets up the class system and the oppression from the very beginning and makes the capitalist system supremely corrupt from the beginning and therefore we must do everything in our power to completely shut it down, so we can be free and our children can be free from it forever.

Working independently we are all forced to suffer the maximum burden of the system designed to keep us down. When we work interdependently we cut the burden in half and by even more. The goal of my Temple is to do exactly that and eventually undermine the system enough to completely break free from it. The people who set up our current system the founding fathers of this country were the worst rich class scum who wanted to escape british and european subjection so they could profit even more and become the masters of their own empire. They promised the people more freedoms and less taxes to get their loyalty to just another exported class system where the elite dominate everything from the top down. I consider anyone who wants to maintain that system to be my enemy. That system must be shut down but maybe not through Marxist methods but more non-violent new age Socialist methods.

All of the current politicians are scumbags even the Socialists ones because they are just as corrupt. If they are not telling us how to escape the capitalist system and how to get rid of the money then they are useless and are only going to perpetuate our poverty slavery.

My system is designed to do just that to use the money collectively against them to eventually get rid of the money and escape the capitalist system altogether.

Peaceful Meditation

Sleep is deep meditation and death is the deepest sleep. Sleep Meditation helps to clear our minds of all the thoughts, pictures, sounds, and clutter that bombards our senses throughout the day and evening. This helps us to be calm, peaceful, and rational. A clear and peaceful mind is a healthy mind. Peaceful Meditation adds even more clarity to our lives. One should practice Peaceful Meditation daily for at least an hour. We must find a peaceful and quiet place where we can relax and sit or lie in silence and empty our minds of all thoughts. We may even dim the lighting or enjoy the outdoors in peaceful tranquility with nature and embracing our solitude where we will find ourselves one with the Universe.

Interdependent Verses Independent

Interdependent means we work together to achieve our needs and goals which is the foundation of my system. This is in opposition of a completely independent system where each individual is responsible for themselves and their own needs and goals. Communal living means that we share the responsibilities, and work duties depending upon our job skills and work assignments. We share ownership of all resources and possessions which is collectively known as Temple Ownership and used based upon an equality and egalitarian method of distribution decided by our Leaders and Temple Regulations. Each Commune however runs its own affairs and economic structure. We encourage others to form Communes and we will have barter and trade between our Communes. One of the main goals is to break free of the capitalist system and we develop strategies to achieve this goal. We work toward a system that does not use money as we know it in the capitalist system. Internal Members have chosen to give up all money and possessions and do their part in the Commune and their reward is having all the luxuries of the Commune because of their service to their people. External Members are Members that choose not to fully become Internal Members and wish to keep their money and possessions but believe in and want to support the Temple, its Ideals, and Goals. External Members donate to the Temple Commune and pay Memberships in support.

The Laveyan system is based upon a complete individual minded independent social and economic structure. Independent systems are mercenary despite any illusions of loyalty to their groups, leaders, or nationalistic beliefs. They are weak structures that will all collapse when the money system becomes unstable and groups and individuals run out of this man made resource. Each person in an independent and capitalist system is responsible for the complete burdens of that system. Living communally cuts those burdens down so that the people can get ahead instead of remaining poverty slaves to the rich class and their corrupt corporations. No mercenary or capitalist system can last long without total brute force and war to subjugate people, take their resources, and put them in debt through poverty slavery and monetary dependence.

Temple of Kama Initiations

The Temple of Kama is accepting those who want to become a Priest or Priestess. A Priest will become a Warrior-Priest and a Priestess a Devadasi-Priestess. Though all can choose the arts they wish to learn and practice. The Priests are also expected to learn the Martial Arts as well as Healing Arts. The Devadasi Priestesses are also expected to learn Dancing, Musical Arts, and Healing Arts which also includes Sexual Healing or Tantric Yoga. You must be 18 to become a Priest or Priestess and be initiated. Both Priests and Priestesses must obviously learn the spiritual religious practices of the Temple. You can bring your own knowledge and practices as well to teach other initiates. You may offer services for free or charge for them but this will depend upon whether or not you or the initiate is an internal or external member.

Communalism the Future

The failures of corrupt Socialism and false Communism may not be understood by most and these are my opinions. First of all there are many forms of Socialism and Socialist type experiments. Many forms failed because of different reasons and some have been successful but undermined by outside powers like capitalism with so-called democratic yet imperial actions.

Let's focus on the Socialism of Russia briefly which is mainly Marxist. First let's understand that Socialism is supposed to be a transition period working toward true Communism. So, Socialism can still have money and a class system. This in my opinion is the very heart of the problem because this automatically perpetuates the corruption of capitalist civilization from the beginning and leads to ultimate failure and a return to capitalism.

Now, let's focus a bit on the Communism of China. First of all true Communism has no monetary system or a class system. Therefore, since China has held onto both of these capitalist aspects from day one their Communist system in spirit was never true Communism, but a form of Socialism which is mainly Marxist. This also leads to failure and a return to capitalism. So, these examples do not truly tell us if Socialism and Communism would work free of the capitalist corruption.

Communalism which has some origins in India and with the Hippy Movement has some Socialist and Communist aspects. My form of Communalism focuses on smaller groups or Communes that are independent but work interdependently. I don't believe in the power of the state or federal authorities trying to control every aspect of our lives and govern or rule over us in the name of the rich class. So, Communalism centers on Decentralization of power down to the village level. This is much like Gandhi's idea of Swaraj or Self-Rule. Most Socialist Parties stand for a Centralization of power but this is the opposite. I also stand for interdependence with a degree of self-efficiency.

Each person in this Temple Commune is a part of the whole machine and expected to do their job or function. Everything is owned by everyone in the Community as a whole. Resources are shared equally and everyone receives their cut of the pie in a sense. Everyone has a job so there is no worry about unemployment. Everyone receives all the basic necessities and needs automatically so they can live and perform their job. No one suffers from unemployment, poverty slavery, starvation, etc. The foundational goal is not based upon profit like in the capitalist system. The foundational goal is based upon simply helping each citizen one hundred percent.

The only real purpose for having a larger federal government is so the rich class can control the people with dominion, taxes, etc. and religious groups can enact and enforce their moral-values through laws. Smaller States, Cities, Towns, Villages, or Communes can run themselves and do not need people from outside trying to dictate their every move. The same problems occur on the smaller levels too but this is why each group can form their own Village or Commune with the systems they choose. The problem is that

the corrupt powers have taken control of all land masses and force everyone to be a subject of their dominion or capitalist system. The solution is to break free from the capitalist system. This can be done through various methods.

One method is to use the capitalist system against itself. We raise the capital to buy our own lands and free ourselves from the burden of rent and buying individual housing. We grow our own food and free ourselves from the expensive and poisoned food markets. We make our own clothing to free ourselves from the corporations machine made clothing, etc. This cuts our burdens in half and down to size! Humans only need to realize their spirituality and interconnectedness. If we surrender our ego and learn to work together then the old saying is truth, "United we stand, divided we fall!"

Caesar's Tantric Hinduism

I want to clear some things up about my religion of Tantric Hinduism which is my own version of similar beliefs. This is a religion that I have created as a parallel and extension of my Spiritual Satanism 999. It is created eclectically using the spiritual and carnal beliefs of traditions I have chosen combined with my own. We do not take the Vedas literally but use them as spiritual guides and for spiritual knowledge. We do not accept Hindu saints, and do not support the Brahmans, or the caste system! This religion is a combination of eastern and western belief systems. Spiritual Satanism 999 has a foundation on the belief of a natural and spiritual war of opposing moral-value systems which also carries over to my Tantric Hinduism! So, let it be known that this is Caesar's Tantric Hinduism! I am the Guru and High Priest of my religion and both Men and Women can become Priests or Priestesses within their own branch. I ask for everyone to please learn more about our belief system and goals. If you would like to support us then contact me or reply. This new religion is still evolving as I learn more and add more to the structure and core of beliefs. I am accepting initiations from new supporters and long established Gurus, Priests, Priestesses, etc. of the left-hand path who would like to help develop, create or contribute traditional rituals, arts, and organize this Temple of Kama.

One Step Closer

Some of you may purely believe in nothing but the Spiritual aspects of religion and see yourselves 10 steps closer to Creation or your Gods. And there are many like myself that are Carnal but believe in combining it with the Spiritual to create a balance. So, is it not better to take 1 step closer to Creation or God than it is to take none at all? So, now the question is will you help us take that 1 step and to fit as much true Spirituality as we can within that 1 step as we will permit? If you agree then will you help us by giving us the Spiritual means to become truly 1 degree more Spiritual. Lend your voice on less moral issues, point out less damning scriptures, give to us more liberal rituals, pujas, mantras, and sadhanas! Offer to us more lenient methods and Guru Discipleship. Present to us egalitarian and classless or caste-less teachings. For this is what I bring to you!

Tantric Yoga, Beginner Lesson 1

The first thing that we must learn is that we are all one being. Your body does not belong to you alone and your mind as well. You are part of a great interconnected system of Spiritual Consciousness and Material Manifestation. We are here for a purpose and that purpose is to do our part in the Spiritual and Material System. We have to learn to first surrender our ego that separates us and to give up our bodies back to the source which is Kali Ma and also Shiva. Through this union we realize that it is against our nature to contaminate our bodies with poisons and toxins. To be overweight and sickly means we have caused great unbalance through our lack of keeping to the Spiritual and Material System. We must bring ourselves to have both an awareness of our oneness and a self-awareness to focus on improving ourselves and our health as well as the health of others in our Temple or group. This path raises spiritual awareness or consciousness to a union with the divine and focuses on becoming physically and spiritually/mentally unbound and free to fulfill our reasonable desires and to engage the divine. There is no moral blockade to achieving fulfillment or to attaining union with the divine. Through this complete self-awareness and the extinction of the self at the same time we allow for the process of physical and spiritual/mental enlightenment. All will be freed in the process becoming unbound and then many will grow tired of the physical aspects and focus more on the spiritual in time.

So, we must learn to be comfortable with our naked selves and our naked union. First begins meditation and Tantric Yoga lessons with clothing on to get used to your group and its union. The next step is to bring in the female Tantric Yogini or Guru. They will remove their clothing so that the group can first experience nudity if they are unaccustomed to this environment. Then they will meditate and perform Tantric Yoga in this fashion. They will grow comfortable in the presence of the naked master. Then the students who are ready to take the next class and higher step, they then will remove their clothing for group meditation and Tantric Yoga lessons. After many classes they will now be ready to take another step and can either engage with a partner or with the master teacher in performing the Meditation and Tantric Yoga Asanas. Those students who need to bring their bodies in balance should also be involved in other forms of Yoga, Ayurvedic Medicine, special vegetarian diet, but we also allow for fish in this Tantric path. All students male and female should learn some Classical Indian Dance and learn Indian Martial Arts or other Martial Arts. All other arts are welcome but the general idea also besides the spiritual aspect is to help maintain a healthy balance which creates the perfect body.

Humans also need sexual fulfillment so Tantric Yoga fulfills this human need as well as brings us into union with Creation, which is more spiritually expressed as the masculine and feminine forces which we also know as deities. Shiva and Kali dance together in mystical union for all eternity! This is Divine Love and it is within us all! We shall learn to give our bodies over to Kali and Shiva and to worship by granting pleasure and fulfillment to all divine humans who also symbolize Shiva and Kali. So, when a devotee seeks such fulfillment from another it is a divine duty and honor to grant such fulfillment to others! The whole concept of denial is what fuels the ego and desires even more. The

majority will never overcome through denial and will remain attached to both the ego and simple desires forever unless we give up an attachment to spreading denial as the only true path. Through allowing as many as possible to fulfill their reasonable desires we free them spiritually/mentally and physically as a result many will then move on focusing on other spiritual disciplines and social works that will free people from poverty slavery, disease, warfare, etc.

9 and the Golden Mean

Interested in more 9 facts or synchronicity? The Golden Mean is 216 which when added equals 9. The Golden Mean was taught by ancients and used in building everything from the Pyramids to Temples, etc. It has been found in atomic particles and dna, etc. If you google it you can find a picture of it in a mathematical spiral design that looks exactly like the 9 and shows a synchronized connection coded into our language. Many believe this has to do with the design or creation of the universe/multiverse and gives credit to dimensional theories, quantum physics, etc. I am no mathematician or physicist but I find the basics intriguing as a Mystic. Also, The Golden Mean/Ratio is much like fractals. You can check the Mandelbrot Set. That's really cool because it's infinite. You can just keep going inward infinitely as the design keeps opening up into new copies of itself smaller and smaller. Try getting stoned and watching one of those. We know that you can multiply 9 by any number and add the digits of the sum and it always equals 9 again. Also, one more thing more basic is when you multiply 9, as the sum goes up to 9(5)=45 it then reverses 9(6)=54, etc. As a bonus multiply this: 111111111(111111111)=

Devadasi Initiation Ritual

The adult woman can choose to become a Devadasi, yet we would like to restore adult age to the age of puberty. This takes place under the full moon and the woman becomes married to the god/goddess Kali-Yellamma and Shiva, other deities, and therefore sadasuhagan. Shiva is a manifestation of the goddess Kali in our Dravidian Matriarchal Shakti system which we also combine with Vamacara or left-hand path Tantra. In our temple we allow our Devadasi to also marry anyone else they wish.

We are missing the full details of this initiation ritual and ask that the Priests and Gurus give to us the remaining details of this ritual ceremony so that we can authentically carry on this practice as close to tradition as possible taking into account our variations and legal blockades.

Traditionally the bride of the god is the god's surrogate also known as the Jogini, offering her services to the Priest and the Priest can direct her to service others. Her main duty and service is to the poor, including sexual services either for free or a low price. Those who can afford to donate to the Temple are expected to as well. The Devadasi should train in one or more arts and crafts. These arts can include courtesan, sexual arts, tantric yoga, classical dancing, singing, instruments, magick arts, healing arts, and in our temple even martial arts, etc. Our Devadasi can choose the men or women she wishes to service and which arts she wishes to practice. In ancient times there were both men and women Devadasi. The Devadasi must be highly respected and honored!

1. Devadasi must be adult women or men.
2. Devadasi can choose other marriage partners.
3. Devadasi can choose which services and arts they wish.
4. Devadasi have equal status with Priests.
5. Devadasi are economically independent but should work interdependently with their Temple.

The Origins of the Devadasi

Hinduism has spawned and influenced many religions from Buddhism, Jainism, Sikhism, etc. but it also has been influenced by outside religions like christianity, islam, and Taoism, etc. Taoism at one point was completely focused on Sexual Practices also known as Joining Energy. This may very well have come out of India with Yoga, Meditation, and Tantra or it may have come into India via Buddhist Tantric Yoga. One thing is certain that for hundreds or even thousands of years Sexual Practices and Sexual Worship of various forms were practiced all over Asia with great acceptance from the Rulers, Priests, Military Elite, and the Common People. During this period or subsequent periods this Sexual Acceptance of Practices and Worship became widespread through India in many forms like Buddhist Yab-Yum or Tantric Yoga, left-hand Vamacara Tantra with Maithuna, and the multiple forms of Holy Whores like the Devadasi, Basivis, Matammas, Venkatasanis, and Joginis! All of these similar traditions of Holy Whores usually practiced other ritualistic arts learned at the Temple much like Buddhists learn knowledge, Tantra, and even Kung Fu. There is also the division between Patriarchal and Matriarchal religions that seems to still be an ongoing battle for control over India. The Brahmin Priestly caste has and is still trying to rewrite history in their own favor. The Shakti Hindu branch seems to be one of those direct Matriarchal Dravidian connections especially with the Kali-Yellamma Order. I see a direct connection of the Holy Whore Devadasi to the ancient Matriarchal Sexual Power and Creation Beliefs or Mythology. When the Buddhist Era in India arose they became associated with Buddhist Nuns and Buddhist Yab-Yum Tantric Yoga which involves Sexual Practices. This means that there was no degeneration from a celibate nun as they had those as well. The Devadasi and many others were not degenerated but elevated over time to even greater heights as Temples were built all over India to glorify them and such practices in the many similar forms under different names. Many even evolving simultaneously yet with separate traditions and probably influencing each other.

The God of Self United With Creation

(Note: This is a letter to a Luciferian.)

I prefer to be called by my author name Caesar. I want to first say that we obviously have our differences. What you are saying is Satanism is only the Laveyan point of view and not from any other source. Satanism as defined by Laveyans has to do with self-godhood. By the way what is wrong with Buddhism? These people are probably the most spiritually advanced on earth and we should be at their feet. I may have a totally different opinion of the Dalai Lama though but that is not relevant to the majority of Buddhists.

I do not believe that traditional Satanism in a basic devil worshipping nature or similar existed before a few hundred years ago if that and probably only by a few christian by day, devil worshippers by night groups. These would be heretical groups in my opinion and not any roots of traditional Satanism, it simply did not exist. There never was a deity called Satan, it was used to describe demonic adversarial forces and spiritual adversaries by judaists and other semitics. There were however plenty of Satanic Archetypes to build upon like Set, etc. though Lucifer, The Light Bringer was not a dark, demonic, or evil deity, but was transformed into one because like many it was just another competing cult for power and the many christian cults especially the catholic cult was not going to stand for it.

I do not use the term Traditional Satanist because I simply do not believe in it but I am a Theistic Satanist and more correctly a Spiritual Satanist. You're idea for the foundation of the LHP comes directly from Laveyan and occult sources but Laveyans were first in trying to make the distinction between their philosophy and devil worshipping religions as a method of building up a monopoly on Satanism. The sheep and wolf scenario is highly Neitchzen another philosopher that I oppose and which Laveyans highly praise. Jesus or his followers use the sheep parable along with many others including the fishing for men parable referring to followers as fish. Are we to not use these parables because they used them? I consider my followers and supporters to be like fish too and sheep. It's just a way to understand the human herd which is good and not something bad. What is bad like you said are some leaders, it doesn't mean that all leaders are bad or that all religion is bad. I'm trying to create a true spiritual religion. It is new age as much as your system of beliefs is new age! My left-hand path is a balance of the spiritual and the carnal as compared to Laveyan beliefs which are completely carnal, selfish, mercenary, capitalist and most right-hand path religions which are completely spiritual, deny the carnal, and some are full of hypocrisy.

You can only define what Satanism is for yourself and when you say that putting the Self last is not Satanism or Satanism is only about the Self-God you are trying to set up a standard for what Satanism is or is not and you simply cannot do that. Your standard is a Laveyan foundation and to me your religion of Luciferian Traditional Satanism is based on Laveyan ideals and not truly spiritual. So, again I see my religion of Satanism 999, (Aka. Vampir Satanism 999, the mystical spiritual name.) as the only true Spiritual Satanism. I present to the world a new or semi-new naturally anti-christian moral-value

system or Satanic Moral-Value System which I've developed from many ancient values that opposed christian values long before they existed or became formalized. We also have a Communal New Age Socialist foundation because we believe the good of the whole is greater than the needs of the individual and the self. We also have my Satanic Trinity of 999 which is a symbolic union of Man, Woman, and Creation.

You Are Not Aristocracy

You are not aristocracy because you had the best education. You are not aristocracy because you are part of the rich class. You are not aristocracy because you belong to the secret orders and clubs. You are not aristocracy because you are a politician or military officer. You are not aristocracy because there is no aristocracy and we are all equal.

Serving Our Temple Society

Our Temple is the structure of our Society. We not only serve our Temple but we must serve our Society and people. This is because the Temple and the Society are one and the same! We serve our Society through doing specific work for our Society and for this we deserve the needs and benefits granted to us that enable us to survive and to be healthy physically and mentally. So, we serve our Society not just for the reward or a profit in capitalism but also to help our people achieve the closest ideal reality to a utopia civilization. This means we help our people achieve or fulfill the needs necessary to make us healthy and happy. The head Priests and Priestesses determine which work and how much work each citizen, each Brother and Sister must do to meet the required standards of work fulfillment. We can supplement Credits in the various communes during our Socialistic transition from capitalism toward our form of Communalism which eventually will no longer use the credit or monetary system within the main Temple Communes that we will represent.

Free Love and the Holy Whore of the Temple of Kama

Free Love is a set of concepts and movements that works to free people from the religious, state, and social groups that regulate and try to enforce religious, state, and social laws that carry the dogma of those associations. Some of the concepts and rights that we support include Sexual Promiscuousness, Anti-Monogamy (A right to be against monogamy or not to be monogamous.), Polygamy, Sexual Equality, Sexual Gifting, Holy Whoredom, Sexual Healing, Homosexuality, Bisexuality, Sodomy, Polyamory, Anti-Age Restrictions (Keeping natural adulthood or recognizing adulthood at an age closer to where nature intended it to be.), etc.

Long before the judeo-christian and islamic moral-values existed and long before intermediate-modern Hindu values (that is from the time the british subjugated India until more recently) there existed other traditions, religions, tribal groups with opposing moral views and values. We can say without a doubt that many (Greek, Roman, Egyptian, Persian, Asian, African, and Native American, etc.)cultures celebrated the joys of sexuality, the Spiritual Sexual Tantra, Sexual Taoism, etc.

In India the Brahmans did hold sway in many areas maintaining Vedanta doctrines, disciplines, and authority. Many of the spiritual stories and values are very beautiful but like many religions the fanaticism can overflow unchecked through time. They became hell bent on maintaining the corrupt caste system and trying to subjugate all other tribes and religious groups in India. Many of these other groups still held more ancient beliefs and opposing moral-values yet also holding many of the same beliefs and interpreting the same spiritual doctrines in a completely different light.

The Devadasi Temple Priestesses were married to the local deity or deities both gods and goddesses. They learned traditional Bharatanatyam dancing and singing, among many other arts including Sexual Healing Arts, Tantra, etc. The dancing and other arts were designed to emphasize many sexual aspects which were later stripped out by Brahmans who once held Devadasi as a far lower caste. The Brahmans had these arts taught to their daughters, wives, etc. They have done this with many arts and practices they considered of lower caste and moral-values. The purpose behind this was to undermine those cultures as they were pushed into minority and out of existence through constant attacks, laws, etc. Then they could present the stripped down arts as their own and claim it as a preservation of Indian Arts.

The Devadasi Temple Holy Whores showed their worship through fulfilling the desires of the divine men, who in return helped support the Temples and the Priestesses. This can be understood through Tantric Beliefs. The divine forces of the masculine and feminine, God and Goddess existed before Creation. They were drawn together by their sacred love and through their divine union all of Creation was born into manifestation. We can understand these forces through many Hindu Deities and sacred stories. Though two pairs of deities can help us understand even more and they are Shiva and Parvati, Krishna and Radha.

First the individual must comprehend their oneness with Creation and so their own divine nature. Then through the practice of ritual reenactments of the divine Creation's copulation we show our worship and love for the Creation, these deities, and ourselves because we are all one. All forms of sexuality become sacred and divine. We raise Kundalini and achieve divine enlightenment and ultimate realization. All through such Tantric Yoga, Meditation, Mantras, Yantras, and Sexual Healing we fill our minds with thoughts of love and spiritual beauty. We embrace our love of Creation, love of Shiva and Parvati, love of Krishna and Radha, love of Divine Men and Divine Women, and ultimately love of our Self. The love of the Deities is the love of ourselves because we are a reflection of these deities and their forces of natures. Within us are the divine masculine and the divine feminine forces of Creation.

Singing and Dancing has always been known by the Gurus as purely divine inspiration and a direct connection to deity within and without. In ancient times many Temples were erected with many types of Temple Holy Whores or Temple Holy Lovers. Some beautiful ancient erotic Tantric Temples can be seen in Khujaho, India. From the Devadasi to modern Flower Children we must keep the Free Love Spirit alive and together we can build Temple's of Kama around the world and beyond our own. Help us support the ancient and modern Devadasi and the Holy Whores of the Temple of Kama. When you're feeling sad and lonely you can give or gift some love and find someone to give or gift to you. When you're feeling depressed and angry think of yourself with your Shiva or Parvati, with your Krishna or Radha and bring some flowers to give to your love and don't forget girls, to put some in your hair.

The Temple of Kama Verses the Feminist

The ultra-feminist is the problem with today's society as they destroy the natural balance that has made traditional human civilization a well-structured, organized, and efficient machine. Women were made very beautiful by nature to pleasure men and have as many babies as possible in order for the race to survive. So, it is important that a majority of women focus on these arts throughout our entire evolution. The feminist has nearly destroyed this harmony and so the races are in decline, the structure of civilization collapsing, the organization lacking, and the efficiency completely eroded.

This has helped to destroy traditional craft and skill services that were divided between the sexes. This has occurred on top of the capitalistic rich class conspiracy to undermine our craft services and skill services in order to force us to rely upon their machines to attain greater wealth and control over the majority of people they breed into their poverty slave class. The feminist's desire to have equality has gone beyond such goals as they seek total domination over men and to free themselves of the traditional crafts and services which has been the foundation of a balanced civilization up until these modern times. This has occurred also as a capitalistic yearning to acquire more personal wealth along with a mercenary independent state. This division of wealth has also helped to destroy the traditional family unit, craft skills, and service skills. Ultimately, the capitalist system has been the diabolic source of this degeneration from our spiritual harmony among the sexes.

It is true that men have become disrespectful and degrading toward women, but this has only been so because the capitalist system is anti-spiritual in itself. This does not excuse women from breaking out of the confines of a harmonious spiritual system designed first by nature and then by the course of human evolution. Men are naturally bigger and stronger for the majority of all races except for maybe a few. This means that men have always been the means of defense in battle, manual labor, hunting, etc. Women have for the majority of races always been the pleasurer, the child barer, the original craft maker clothing, etc., probably farming, and original spiritual priestesses and healers. This spiritual center would surround their sacred art of the holy whore to please men, bare children, perform seasonal ceremonies in devotion to the gods and goddesses, etc. So, traditionally the art of the sexual prostitute was sacred and probably free or based upon simple trade in the temple until capitalism became a corrupted form of traditional barter.

There is nothing wrong with such arts, but christians, judaists, and muslims, will all try to tell you there is something wrong. It's not degrading until the respect is lost through such anti-teachings and opposing values, or very ignorant men that show no respect for the women or such professions. These people are the ones that need to be outcast for their idiot culture that is usually based in some modern anti-spiritual sport mentality. Most feminists seem to be coming from such religious backgrounds and carry with them the same form of moral-value system. The few truly liberal feminists may not be the heart of the problem if at all. Essentially equality is not an issue for our Temple. It is the feminist that helps to undermine such traditional roles that have helped civilization advance and

originally helped us from being enslaved by such mega controlling greed driven super-rich capitalists.

In our Temple we invite the women to first explore their traditional purpose in life which is basically to please men and make babies. This is a sacred Spiritual Priestess Path and not something degrading. This is also done as a traditional form of worship of these Creation gods and goddesses. Those women who do not find this path in harmony with their nature are free to pursue other paths, since equality and true freedom are something that we do also encourage. The feminist with her modern beliefs has made it quite difficult to present and practice our spiritual religious path as it was practiced in ancient times. The ideal would be to have thousands of Priestesses performing these arts openly, liberally, and respectably in the Temples as once was the tradition in many parts of the world. The male Warrior-Priests would practice their martial arts and other spiritual training in their own Temples and would visit these Holy Whores as often as needed to keep civilization's morale high and a balance maintained.

In order to rebuild our ancient civilization gathering from many traditions rather than just one we will have to break free of the capitalist system, undermine the judeo-christian moral-value system, break the pride of the ultra feminist, and re-instill the special form of spirituality of our Temple within the mass of our followers and children. This is a declaration of war between opposing moral-value systems in a time of overall disintegrating spirituality in general. Those who support the judeo-christian moral-value system or anything similar even if they are not judeo-christian are the social enemies of our Temple of Kama.

Awaken the Spiritual Health Consciousness

Natives were never fat until they were forced to eat white people food, alcohol, and forced on to reservations. Natives were always very spiritual and healthy people. And I feel so bad about what has happened to Natives. There is something wrong with being fat it's a disease and part of other diseases. It's very unhealthy and I won't ever approve of it or say that it's ok to be fat. Even being chubby is not healthy as it is the beginning of becoming fatter and we have to teach people to catch it and change their lifestyle while they still can. Humans are not supposed to have fat on their bodies that bulges out anywhere. The food today is even worse than ever before. They are poisoning everyone with foods that are causing the fat disease, diabetes, heart disease, cancer, etc. None of the standard foods in supermarkets are natural or healthy and people need to be awakened to this reality. Most people are so ignorant to the facts or don't care and poison their children and themselves because they think the government is going to tell them the truth about it. The government has been lying and deceiving the population for generations especially about the food. The big food corporations make hundreds of millions of dollars a year and millions of that goes into the political parties, etc. They will never tell the truth until decades after when many generations are dead or half dead. The only way to be partially safe is to eat 100% natural and nothing in the supermarkets have anything 100% natural. Natives are being hit very hard by the same deception with the food and I'm not even sure if they realize it yet.

I try not to eat anything that is not whole grain, because processed foods are what is causing these diseases along with not enough exercise. The food now is so bad that even exercise is making it impossible to lose weight. They also have us programmed to eat like 10 times more than we need to eat. Food with processed grains allow our bodies to digest almost all of the food very quickly which spikes our blood sugar super high then we crash and are still hungry and want more food. When it's super high this causes insulin to be released to stabilize our blood sugar or we go into a coma. This can happen dozens of times a day as long as we eat that processed food and over time this helps cause insulin resistance and diabetes. This also causes us to gain weight because it tries to store the excess sugar. Now, high fructose corn syrup is far worse than processed sugar cane. This stuff destroys the liver like alcoholic disease and the liver stores almost all of it as fat. The body can't use high fructose corn syrup as fuel until it's converted to fat, after the glycogen stores are filled. People eat so much of it that they are filled quickly and the rest is constantly going to fat to make us fat diseased, helps cause diabetes too, etc. Being overweight is a major factor in diabetes, as is liver destruction, not exercising, etc.

For example a bowl of whole grain rice with some beans would be great for a whole day. This is because whole grain is digested slowly and therefore releases sugar slowly throughout the day. This also gives you a full feeling and you don't spike your blood sugar so high. This is why natural unprocessed food is healthy food and processed food is not healthy. Now, to fight cancer we need to eat organic. No pesticides, herbicides, antibiotics, or hormones added to the food. And no gmo or genetically modified foods but mostly everything is today. I'm not against the gmo, just they don't test it. They are testing it by feeding it to us and then see the results after years of us eating it. Humans are

not supposed to eat any dairy but mother milk when we are little. They have us brainwashed into thinking we need to eat it. Drinking the milk causes osteoporosis from the acidic levels caused by the high protein. The high fat count in dairy from the fatty food they feed them instead of letting them graze naturally on grass. Anyhow that helps cause heart disease, etc. Again they put hormones, antibiotics in the diary and meat. They also irradiate much of the meat, this adds more radiation that causes cancers. I don't eat any meat, just seafood. Even that is getting contaminated. I don't eat anything fried or any form of processed vegetable oils. This stuff is horrible contributing to almost all major diseases. If one must have a little oil, then cold pressed extra virgin olive oil. Someone has to save us and our children. I consider my job as a spiritual priest and healer to do it.

Another thing they are adding to everything is salt. This is poison! It causes high blood pressure, heart disease, kidney failure, extreme swelling in the legs, etc. All of it has to be processed out. Humans can't take any added salt in the diet, only what is naturally locked in foods. This salt is not natural sea salt either. Sea salt is far better cause it has over 100 trace minerals we need and we get less of the actual salt. The salt they put in everything in processed food is processed. It comes from mines deep in the earth then is purified and all other minerals removed. They then add titanium and iodine. We have no need for these. Titanium is a poisonous metal to humans and we only need small traces of natural iodine not their processed garbage. Iodine is what they give to people during nuclear fallout or radiation poisoning. People gobble down tons of salt and wonder why they have high blood pressure, kidney failure, and swelling legs, etc. The body can't remove it all fast enough and as kidneys fail from trying to remove it constantly it has to remove it from the blood and so stores it under the skin with water. As usual the quack doctors put people on tons of drugs for high blood pressure etc., and they don't need this crap, it only kills them faster. The doctors and pharmaceutical companies are non-spiritual people that only care about money and career opportunities. They are not true spiritual healers! We are slowly being poisoned to death so that huge corporations can profit and for population control. I don't consider this freedom. I consider it enslavement and elimination through idiocy and spiritual degeneration.

Here is another huge problem. They are now fortifying every standard product with vitamins and minerals. The problem is that most of these are chemically produced in a lab, they are not natural and they have no idea of the real amounts we need in combination with other natural ones! The other problem is that they are in most cases the wrong kind, being inorganic instead of organic or coming from natural food sources. The body needs these organic forms not the inorganic forms and so we can be deficient of a vitamin and at the same time be overdosing on the same one because it's useless to us and we are unable to deal with it. I don't want anything created in a lab to be put in my body or my children if I ever had any. I probably will never have kids. The worst place to ever have kids is in the u.s. They are giving half of them cancer through population control methods and force parents to give them chemotherapy treatments which is one of the causes of cancer not a cure! If the parent believes in any other form of non-mainstream medicine the courts try to take your kid and force them to get chemotherapy. I've never heard of this in any other country. They are giving us cancer in many ways, like the

vaccinations, food, etc. They also give them autism, etc. Anyhow I stay away from all foods that are fortified and would never give them to my kids, again if I had them.

Real quick to touch on another subject, they are putting dangerous preservatives in everything that cause all sorts of problems and contribute to a host of diseases. These unnatural preservatives must be avoided as well. The government, the mainstream quack doctors, and pharmaceutical companies are all trying to maintain a monopoly on health care and so try to keep other forms of medicine limited and unable to claim certain cures or preventions of disease. They also have a vigorous system for controlling natural herbs and substances they call drugs so that they can control the market on these things too and it has far less to do with making sure people are safe. Their kind of medicine focuses on using drugs for cures or to relieve symptoms which never addresses or removes the real problems and expect people to take their drugs forever. Their drugs only make people sicker and kill them faster. Real Traditional Medicine focused on prevention and spirituality. It would still be mainstream if it wasn't forced to the side by legal restraints! India has some advanced systems like Ayurveda, Siddha, etc. Chinese and other Asians have advanced herbal medicines. Natives from all over had advanced herbal and spiritual medicine systems but far little is left but some are making a comeback.

What We Do Not Need

1. We do not need college.

College is for the rich and upper middle class to use as some sort of class job segregation between blue collar and white collar workers. They brain wash the people into this fantasy that they need more money, to own their own homes, their own cars, etc. This only perpetuates the poverty class slavery that exists. Also, these colleges cost a fortune when they should be free. They also dictate facts to students in crammed over populated classes and expect the student to learn at a fast pace or get left behind. This is the wrong form of learning which many cannot deal with and fall through the system. The best form of learning is self-learning which was advocated by many including Timothy Leary. The private college industry must be shut down!

2. We do not need to own automobiles.

We do not need to buy their automobiles, pay their gas prices, their auto insurance, registration, inspection, driver's licenses, etc. This is another huge racket that we do not need to buy into literally. We need to put an end to the entire fossil fuel industries as well as the auto industries which work together. Transportation can and eventually will be free when we overthrow this broken and sinister economic system.

3. We do not need to own homes.

We do not need to buy their houses or even pay steep rent. We are being inculcated with their fantasies of dream homes and living lavish lifestyles that only contribute to our abundant miseries under a rich class and upper middle class hell bent on staying in power forever which as a consequence maintains a much larger poverty slave class forever. The housing industry must be abandoned and left behind in this new world system. People spend half their lives or more paying off mortgages on something so incredibly impermanent. They think they really truly own something in this diabolic system. If you must pay endless taxes or some sort of licensing fee then you truly do not own it. Also, all land and resources belong to all people collectively and can never belong to one person or one group alone. So, in the end anything you think you own in this imaginary system of capitalism will eventually return to the collective. The housing industry will burn to the ground literally as the economy self-implodes over and over.

4. We do not need to own excessive amounts of new clothing.

We do not need excessive amounts of new clothing. This is some kind of futile desire which helps to keep millions of people in rags worldwide. Why do these people insist on desiring to have more than they can possibly need to get by? It's because they are little primitive children full of unchecked greed. We as a people must put them in check and make sure all people have the proper amount of clothing fit for survival. People again are being inculcated from the time of childhood to desire tons of fancy glamorous clothing which they do not truly need. This excessiveness is quite the sickness as they are

bombarded constantly by advertisements, commercials, new clothing lines, etc. To make it even worse the wealthy and middle class have worked to undermine the craft skills of the workers introducing machines to control everything and for them to save money competing with craft workers. Through this they force the craft workers to lose their skills and become super cheap labor in their labor market camps and sweat lodges. This upper class industry must be eradicated and people's excessive desires for myriads of clothing stifled through spiritual education and enlightenment. The greed mongers will be outcast and bred off into extinction.

5. We do not need to own money.

Finally, we do not need to own money of any kind. This is the biggest fantasy that they inculcate people with in the capitalist system. It's the most important method for them to control the people and keep you under their control and power through class segregation. We live in a capitalist system that was designed and created by the rich class to maintain their authority perpetually. Do not let them try to tell you anything different, because they will lie ceaselessly in order to look like some kind of beneficial service to humanity and even worse some kind of benevolent authority or great providence. The upper middle class and rich class are truly the most loathsome, disgusting, corrupt, egomaniacal, self-centered, degenerate, conniving, ruthless people on the face of the earth. It would truly be a divine grace if they were all just wiped out and eliminated from the planet suddenly and eternally. They can take their money with them into the negative veil of existence because we simply do not need it to function and thrive. Ultimately, the capitalist system will perish in its fiery demise and the people will be freed from the tyranny of its oppressive regime.

The Courtesan Verses the Temple of Kama Holy Whore

Any woman who acquires wealth in any form i.e. gifts, purchases, transactions, money, etc. while in a relationship and does not return these forms of wealth when the relationship ends is a courtesan. Any woman who acquires wealth through the process of ending a relationship, marriage, etc. in the form of a legal separation, divorce settlement, etc. is a courtesan. A courtesan is a higher class of prostitute who is well educated and trained in this art form which includes the deception of men to acquire wealth. Courtesans provide sexual fulfillment, companionship, entertainment, fulfill the fantasy of love, fulfill the fantasy and relationship status of bride or groom, etc. We are not against such art forms, beliefs, or practices, etc. We simply wish to educate men and even women who would be fooled by such women or men because of their foolishness, naivety, and fantasies. There are also male courtesans but the majority are women. These women or men will go so far as wedding, and having children with these men or women to acquire as much wealth as possible. As a man I speak mostly to men and they should be wise to these women and their agenda. You would be better off in most cases to just visit the basic prostitute to eliminate the deception, unless you were fully aware of the fantasy role of such women and enjoyed this experience far more. My Temple highly respects the Holy Whore or Sacred Prostitute who openly worships the Gods and Goddesses of Creation through fulfilling men and women's sexual desires which is reflected in their own godhood. We have very little to no respect for those that deceive for wealth alone! So, the courtesan that deceives is a lower class in our Temple. The courtesan that makes her intentions open and clear has far more respect. The Holy Whore has the highest respect and honor for her sacred art and profession!

The Final Reality

It doesn't matter which pill you take because everything we think is reality will eventually be shattered.

The final reality to be shattered is life. We create or come to believe in elaborate fantasies or other realities about life beyond this life. I believe in a form of reincarnation. I also believe that higher and higher realities exist, like awakening from a dream. If we can dream and be convinced that it is real, then what is to say that this waking world is not just an even more powerful dream state? The idea for the matrix is actually based upon theoretically possible science, though science is only a small aspect of understanding this world in relation to our method of comprehending and consciousness. I don't see it as any absolute truth or it would just be another dogma based religion. Reality as we know it I feel changes with our consciousness which is a reflection of the Great Consciousness of Creation. So, even science will bend, twist, and be rewritten, recalculated, and re-understood for each generation as their consciousness and perceptions of reality changes. The minds of the people and their Science and Spirituality/Religion will eventually merge as they both achieve higher levels of conscious reality and understanding.

The Sacred First Purposes of Men and Women/
Women Exist For Two Main Purposes in Life

Women Exist for two main purposes in life. The first purpose is to procreate or create babies to multiply the race and insure survival of the species. This includes raising the children. This brings us to the second purpose. Women's beauty is designed to attract mainly male partners to pleasure them and as a result create babies. Therefore, the second purpose of Women's Existence is to pleasure men and also other women.

Practice pleasuring among themselves helps them to learn to pleasure men even more which will only add to the survival of the race. Ironically, men can practice pleasuring among themselves too to help them learn to better pleasure the woman as part of their purposes in life. Men's sacred first purposes are first procreation and second protection of the women and children.

Women and Men should not be taught that there is something wrong with these purposes and should be taught to proudly fulfill these purposes. Though neither sex should feel bound to these purposes but should fully embrace them if they choose to. Women can choose any career path and are not obligated to pursue specific arts or careers. The point is that there is nothing wrong with fulfilling nature's purposes that have been given to us. There is nothing shameful or sinful about having babies or pleasuring many men or even women.

Don't let the feminist tell you that it is degrading or let the Christian, Judaist, Muslim, Hindu, Wiccan, Atheist, or even a Satanist look down upon you with their dogma. Creation designed you specifically to be so beautiful that many would desire your pleasure and create many babies with you. Though nature would have had the strongest and wisest make you their own and possibly share you with their clan brothers. In modern times the difference is that you can now decide and choose your partners because of laws.

Nature never intended for there to be marriage and monogamy. This undermines your purposes in life. Nature made most women smaller and weaker than men because the men were supposed to do the main labor jobs, mate, hunt, fight, defend, build, etc. Women were supposed to do the easier jobs, receive mating, raise children, forage, pick berries, sew, cook, clean, farm, etc. In areas where women were big as or bigger than men, the roles would have been equal or even switched.

The majority of races were designed with women being much smaller than men. This set the standards for many generations of traditional roles. There is nothing wrong with those roles if you want to practice them. If everyone stopped practicing the roles we were meant to practice then all of our traditions upon which civilization are built will be lost and civilization will crumble. What will be left is a civilization that has no gender specific roles, no traditions, and a high crime rate from the lowest morale in human history. As long as Christian and feminist based values exist, sway, and contaminate society then the majority of men will have a lowered morale and civilization will be plunged back into the dark ages.

Even when female Priestesses controlled the Temples of Civilization during the matriarchal period, the traditional roles existed because this is how humans are genetically formed and programmed. Women made the final decisions of many spiritual and ritualistic problems and followed a High Priestess Alpha Woman. There also would have been an Alpha Male Chief. Their spiritual union would seal the peace and balance the authority. This certainly would not have been a monogamous marriage because why would they want something that would limit their powers, pleasures, and abilities? Only more modern religions have developed such degrading spiritual virtues and values. We also must not equate modern with being more spiritually advanced.

What defines spiritual advancement? I define it as freedom from limitations that deny us pleasures that can do us or others no harm. I define it as having the power to fulfill others desires as well as our own. I define it as not allowing ego to inflict suffering on others. I define it as equality without denying our true purposes in life. I define it as helping fulfill others before ourselves when it is realistically possible. I define it as not becoming jealous, not being greedy, not being possessive, not deceiving, not injuring, and not fighting.

The idea is to continue to work toward such high ideals even if it is unrealistic. Therefore, the goal is to come close to our ideals. The women of our Temple are encouraged to gloriously fulfill their sacred first purposes in life. Women are encouraged to follow Creation's Divine Copulation and create babies and to pleasure as many men and women as they can. Men are also encouraged to fulfill their sacred first purposes. Here we help to define the sacred nature of our Tantric Nature-Sex Religion.

Tribal Clans and Monetary Systems

Colleges are only a way to bleed your personal fortunes and build independent lifestyles that undermine Socialist Values that free you from capitalist mercenary poverty slavery and exploitation. Men should focus on Warrior-Priest Training, Craft Making, Services, etc. While Women should focus more on Priestess Training, Child Baring/Raising, Craft Making, Services, and Healing Arts. If there is to be any form of wealth in your Clan, then you should focus on Clan Wealth and not the wealth of the individual. The good of the Clan comes before the individual at all times. Those without a Clan become their own Clan by default. Traditional Barter Trade is encouraged between Tribal Clans. The purpose of developing self-efficient skills is to free you and your people from becoming unskilled workers enslaved to the capitalist wage and class system which is a system of exploitation and leaves thousands at the mercy of an unstable system facing mass unemployment and severe poverty as a result of being dependent upon their monetary units. The truth is we do not need their monetary or class system. We do not need to be enslaved to their class system or their money. We must not let their rich class politicians brainwash us into believing that we need them or their capitalist system. This is only a way for them to control us like cattle and live luxurious lives as the majority of us live in a state of complete poverty slavery. Their elite rich-class controls all aspects of civilization and religion and so becomes the goal of major religions like christianity to maintain control through this form of capitalist system. So, controlling the politics becomes a full time task for these people where they invest billions into this priority of theirs. How else can they keep themselves in the wealthy class and ruling class? If we reject their monetary system and develop our own skills to become self-sufficient within our own Clans then they become powerless over us and fall from their wealthy class positions both economically and politically. Their money won't be worth the paper it is printed on!

Haunted River

There was this river and it looked kind of swimmable on the surface but sometimes you can see it was quite current-y or fast or tricky and it was nice, all around it trees, grass, etc. It was fairly wide and had what looked like a normal current usually on surface, but it was kind of dark. Anyhow I was standing by this river and it looked beautiful and kept calling to me in a way kind of like saying come swim in me cool off. Because it seemed like hot summer day. Strangely I started seeing like ghostly little girls that would run out and jump into it all happily. The girls ranged from real young to older and from both sides. Then I was seeing scenes of them being sucked under and cemetery scenes all while the river was still there. It went from a happy scene to macabre kind of eerie feeling and strangely I still felt drawn to it. I kept stepping closer and closer to the edge and looking down into it cause I was seeing these visions from it and it felt pleasant and then scary at the same time, though both feelings seem to grow at once. Then suddenly I either jumped in or fell in, I couldn't tell, seemed like both. Then I realized that the current was insanely horrible and no one could escape it, especially a little girl. I continued to see the drowning girls as they jumped in overtime and the horror on their faces once that bore sweet smiles as they happily jumped in to cool off. I was being sucked under as I tried to fight this monster of a current. There was nothing to grasp, to even try to escape. You were completely powerless and in the jaws of this beast. It seemed to be feeding on more than our flesh, but our souls. I was thinking a tree, a thick tree I saw it was like 6-7 inches wide and round. I somehow managed to grab it at the edge. I pulled first on one of its roots but it was slipping and then I grabbed the trunk. I used all of my strength to pull myself from this ravaging, thunderous, ensnaring torrent. Then I looked back upon its grave mysteries and screaming lost souls one last time. Mhahahahhahaah, but still it echoes through my mind as I still see its demonic beauty as I am surely awake.

Diwali 2010

Each year Diwali is set by the position of the Moon or New Moon. This year it will be celebrated on Nov. 5, 2010. This date varies throughout India and the Holiday takes place over 5 days. Each day has a Traditional Name and celebrates and worships different deities and or associated mythologies or beliefs. Also, different rituals and customs are carried out. These differ from location to location but mainly are just a northern and southern difference. It is far more intricate than can be explained briefly here. I encourage everyone to do your own research.

There are several deep mythological and truly believed events that have brought about the Diwali Celebrations and Worship. This entails a good prevailing over evil scenario where the Avatar of Lord Krishna defeated the evil demon Narakasura. Another scenario is Lord Rama defeating the demon king Ramana. My favorite aspects of this holy festival are more of the esoteric beliefs than the colorful, beautiful, and moral narratives with respective deities. Here is an excerpt explaining some of the more esoteric meanings behind Diwali.

"While Deepavali is popularly known as the "festival of lights", the most significant esoteric meaning is "the awareness of the inner light".

Central to Hindu philosophy, is the assertion that there is something beyond the physical body and mind which is pure, infinite, and eternal, called the Atman. Just as we celebrate the birth of our physical being, Deepavali is the celebration of this Inner Light, in particular the knowing of which outshines all darkness (removes all obstacles and dispels all ignorance), awakening the individual to one's true nature, not as the body, but as the unchanging, infinite, immanent and transcendent reality. With the realization of the Atman, comes universal compassion, love, and the awareness of the oneness of all things (higher knowledge). This brings Ananda (Inner Joy or Peace).

Deepavali celebrates this through festive fireworks, lights, flowers, sharing sweets, and worship. While the story behind Deepavali varies from region to region, the essence is the same - to rejoice in the Inner Light (Atman) or the underlying reality of all things (Brahman)."

Church/Temple Memberships

External Church Memberships are $100 per year for anyone who makes under $50,000 per year and a tithe or one tenth of their salary for anyone who makes over $50,000 per year. Internal Memberships are free as long as Internal Members complete their Temple Jobs.

Churches and Temples around the world collect billions of dollars in tithes from their loyal supporters to keep them going and in some countries the state pays the Churches and Temples through citizen taxes. If they can put so much support into their Churches and Temples, so can our people and supporters. We will need to rise to their level of commitment to overcome their persistent attack of our rights and counter-values. Our long term goal is to eventually break away from the capitalist system and its monetary use to create a Temple Nation without borders. We will allow people from all classes to join us if they pay their tithe and support our long term and short term goals, beliefs, and principles.

Chant Jai Kali Ma

Here is a short list of Temple activities.

1. Kali Ritual Puja. (Day and Tantric Night Rituals!)

2. Chanting: Jai Kali Ma! (Other Chants!)

3. Music: ♪ ♫ (Indian Classical Music, etc.!)

4. Dance: Bharatanatyam (Restored with the full erotic sexual aspects, topless, and more revealing outfits! Also, other forms of dance, Indian Classical Styles, Belly, etc.!)

5. Meditation, Yoga, Tantric Sexual Yoga, Other Healing Arts, etc. (Different Days!)

6. Vegetable and Fruit Feast! (Vegetarian and Fish in Tantric)

Ka-Ma

Ka is short for Kali and Ma is short for Mother. Together they make the word Kama which also means Divine Love and Divine Sex! Open your minds and hearts to the Temple of Kama! Hail Kali Ma! Hail Kali-Yellamma!

Praise to Dark Goddess Mother

Kali is the Supreme Deity of the Living Creation, the Universal Consciousness. She is the Supreme Brahman. She is the Divine feminine force, Shakti! From Kali all other gods and goddesses take form. From Kali all of Creation is born from her union with Shiva her consort. This is the Vamacara (Left-Handed Path). This includes Pujas, Kali Puja, Sadhana (Spiritual and Ritual Practice) including Kama Mudra (Tantric Yoga), Madya (Consecrated Wine), Matsya (Consecrated Fish), Mantras (Alphabet, etc.), Meditation (Emptiness, Focus, Peaceful), Traditional Indian Dancing, etc. Also, the study and practice of Healing arts, Martial Arts, and Magickal Arts.

Jai Kali Ma!

Praise to Dark Goddess Mother!

Hail the Body and Spirit of Existence

Life is too short just have a good time and forget about too many strict moral-values! Indulge in the pleasures of life! Let your worship be filled with pleasures too. Hail Kali Ma! Hail the body and the spirit of existence!

Give Love and Pleasure

Your people need both love and pleasure. Give these things to your people and make them happy. Your body is not just your body, it is the body of your People and Creation. It is your duty to share your love and your pleasure. I am your Guru, your Teacher, and my chosen name is Caesar.

More on Spiritual Satanism 999

My system is still fairly new after 10 years since I first started spreading my beliefs. I was around before some of these other groups claiming to be Spiritual Satanism or Theistic. I didn't use those terminologies back then, just considered myself to be more of the traditional branch but some have been working to further define those terminologies since that time. I can say I know of some women and several groups who have been trying to define what Spiritual Satanism is and is not for their own benefit. What I believe is my own form or branch and I don't claim it to be the definition of all or a so-called true Satanism in the theistic or spiritual branch like many of them do. I do think my branch is the only truly spiritual branch because I have not found others with the same spirituality and religious piety.

In my system Satan is one of many names and aspects of gods and goddesses that I accept which represent Creation. Satan represents more of the Adversarial aspect of Creation and I believe Creation to be its own Adversary. This Creation is a Universal Consciousness. The only deity we do not accept and deny is the abrahamic god of judaists, christians, and muslims. Therefore, my religion is polytheistic, monotheistic, and pantheistic, etc. We can have branches devoted to various deities and beliefs that do not contradict our own. This is why I have also been developing another spiritual system as a parallel to my Satanism 999. This parallel system is basically known as my form of Tantric Hinduism which has left-hand path Tantric and Matriarchal Shakti beliefs, etc.

There are several main doctrines in my system with many more smaller ones of less importance. The most important doctrine is our anti-christian or Satanic Moral Value System which is a semi-new system which I've developed from many ancient cultures that had beliefs that opposed the judeo-christian moral value system long before it existed or enforced its dogma by authoritarian methods. Another doctrine is my Satanic Trinity of 999. This symbolizes the Divine Marriage between Man, Woman, and Creation. This is also our Satanic Creation for those who relate better with that Adversarial Nature. These are some very basic outlines to give you an idea of my deep Spiritual System.

Tiamat and the Recruitment Process

There seems to be a problem in the recruitment process. What I'm trying to do is to find people with two mind sets in one. The first mind set is that of the person with the naturally occurring anti-christian mental view. I compare this to the new or semi-new complete detailed anti-christian moral-value system I have created. This new anti-christian system can be found in my Satanic Bible for our people and development. The second mind set is that of the interdependent and self-sacrificing mentality. It is important that our people think of the good of the whole group and this means specifically our own group, people, or family.

When I search among the mainly anti-spiritual and Satanic who readily agree with many of the anti-christian values I represent I find that they are also naturally selfish and mercenary. This is a fact Lavey was well aware of when he decided to capitalize off of their natural primitive state of mind. Then when I search among those who have entered a higher spiritual development they have already been inculcated by the judeo-christian moral-value system or one similar in connection to another religion. These people are highly against the values that we represent and they work hard to make practices surrounding those values illegal. This is the root of the oppression which they spread based upon their dogma. Those religions when not trying to exterminate each other, work together for support much like the rich classes of different countries work together to maintain the corrupt capitalist system in as many regions of the world as they can.

I represent the only true form of Spiritual Satanism that is in complete contrast to Laveyan Satanic principles and beliefs. The Laveyan is mercenary to the core while atheistic religiously. This system is one I highly oppose because I am truly a very spiritually centered being and theistic. In my system Satan is only one name for the forces that exist in nature and can be called Creation, Universe, Logos, Word, God, Goddess, etc. There can be multiple names and multiple deities or all can be one.

Laveyans despise religion in general and work against it in a futile and false quest. So, in reality they represent only the business of capitalizing upon those they claim to inspire. The Alien Elite will never rise from the shadows of christian dominion. The truly Spiritual Satanist will conquer all bonds in time. Then we will no longer wander simply among the shadows and cold distant borders but we will ascend the seats of strength and glory, triumphant in the light of day yet always remain masters' of the night.

Mercenaries will capitalize upon each other like the endlessly feeding rodents of a cesspool of filth and sludge. When the Spiritual Mind awakens it becomes determined to unite and fight toward their goal unrelenting. The idealist cannot be defeated by a realist view because the universe is idealist and spiritual by nature. It is the fanaticism that we must always be ever aware of within ourselves in order to keep it in check. This has been a great issue sparking fear deep in the hearts and minds of these realists. They live in fear of their spiritual selves and opening the door to its endless possibilities because of the sleeping serpent Tiamat which lies dormant within us all and the universe.

It is the christian oppressors among many others who we see in these modern times who dare to summon and awaken the awesome powers of Tiamat through their own fanaticism and oppression of other peoples and their beliefs. The hypocrisy they breed throughout the ages has caused more suffering than would have existed without them. They tempt the scales of judgment with a blackened heart against a divine feather. If Tiamat awakens then all hope may be lost because Pandora's Box will be torn open when the Storm is released.

Fight for Your Rights against Judeo-Christian Oppression

Do you have any idea of the rights they strip away from us through civil laws based upon their moral-values? It's a very passive aggressive form of oppression. They talk about peace and love of god, jesus, etc., then condemn many things they find offensive to their own values and beliefs which they claim as the only truth. This dogma cannot be allowed to be enforced through local, state, and federal government, yet it is because they simply are the majority and they work hard to control the government. This is a partnership with the rich class and the capitalist system in general. If you look at the laws they work to maintain and work to pass even more they are all based upon their religious interests and moral-values. For example: 1. Gay rights to marriage and military service. They teach that being gay is wrong/immoral and sick. Laws exist to ban it and working to ban it further and change the constitution. 2. The right to pander and prostitute. They teach that it's immoral and degrading. Laws have existed on this for a long time, which only empower the black market. 3. The right to abortion, polygamy, just to be promiscuous, etc., etc., etc. I see this as a war of opposing moral-values. Christians, judaists, muslims, etc., all claim their values and god are the only truth and will kill to enforce it. So, you should now see why I consider them my enemies. The majority of christians will vote for whoever supports enforcing their values into law. So, each christian that willingly votes is oppressing my rights and the rights of my people and therefore are my enemies by nature. I'm a very spiritual human being but I'm not going to respect nor give any alliance to people who overtly and covertly work to oppress my people and myself. The problem has been that most people who have been told by christians that they are immoral do not have the understanding yet that they are not immoral but simply hold opposing moral views and must gain the confidence to stand by them, practice, and teach them. This is what I do, I teach the outcasts from christian civilization to feel secure in the knowledge that they are not wrong or immoral and must fight for their rights on a social level!

Spiritual Antichrist on Earth

I am the chosen representative symbolic Spiritual Antichrist on Earth, the High Priest and Supreme General/Commander of my Church of the Antichrist 999. I was called upon by my concept of Satanic Creation to be the Spiritual Leader of my People, and bring a New Liberal Theistic Satanic Religion! It is based on a semi-militant form of organization.

Worker Charkha or the Wheel of Workers

1. The Farmers

They grow the needed fruit, vegetables, rice, cotton, dye plants, spices, etc.

2. The Spinners

They spin the yarn needed to make the clothing, etc.

3. The Clothing Makers

They make all the clothing, etc.

4. The Food Preparers

They prepare the food, water, etc.

5. The Craft Workers

They make all the crafts, and building work.

6. The Teachers

They teach all arts, crafts, knowledge, etc.

7. The Satyagraha Army (non-violent)

They train to be non-violent soldiers to secure our rights and freedom.

8. The Priest/ess Healers

They perform all the different religious ceremonies, meditate, give spiritual advise, and perform healing arts of various kinds.

9. The Musicians and Dancers *New

They learn, practice, play, perform, and teach all forms of music and dance.

10. The Service Workers *New

They are all other types of service workers.

Caesar's Ashram Project

Caesar's Ashram Project is designed to raise money for our Temple Ashram. We accept donations, your volunteer services, your support, and membership. Caesar's Ashram is the core of our Temple foundation. It will provide healing and spiritual services to both our members and those outside our community that wish to pay for our services and projects. You may have seen the Workers Charkha, which our Temple Ashram will be based upon. This is a microcosm within the macrocosm of the world community which may participate in our Worker Charkha. Meaning that outside members that follow the pattern of our Worker Charkha can trade with our main Temple of Kama Ashram, and other Temples, Ashrams, Communes, etc. Those that join our Temple Ashram will devote their energies and time toward developing and expanding our Ashram in the name of our Creation Consciousness. We are here to help our people find unity with Creation, to heal them, and to develop proper living values and environment according to our unique Dharma. This means that those who join our Temple Ashram do so not for personal benefit besides true freedom, securing our rights, Swaraj, improved health, well-being, self-perfection, and peace of mind. Those that seek to profit can reside outside of our Ashram becoming part of the larger World Ashram, and may trade with our community, etc. Contact me if you are interested in joining and helping out with my Ashram.

Caesar's Swaraj

I don't like college much. I follow the beliefs of Dr. Timothy Leary, and others who have shown us that mainstream schools just brainwash us by making us copy their facts, instead of learning ourselves. Self-learning, smaller schools, and trade schools are much better. His motto was "Turn on, tune in, and drop out." He was a professor during the hippy counter culture movement of the 60's. And if schools are free it's even better. Schools are so expensive. Most poor people can't afford them. I believe all school should be free.

I want to build my temple like a big commune society. And everyone helps out, making crafts, and providing services, etc. So, a college degree is not necessary, etc. People share the responsibility and that's very equality driven. I didn't even go to high school that long. I dropped out, though I went back for my diploma at night school later on. Most of what I know, I taught myself. I don't think it's important that people have to go to college, and I would like to see them save their money for better things, join me, or invest in my temple, where they would always have a home and a position. But if that's what they really want, to go to college, then that's ok too. But it sure doesn't help my temple and our people, unless they come join me later on.

The idea is a group of people working interdependently together will reduce the capitalist burdens the rich class puts on the poverty slave or worker class. Being totally independent in a capitalist system makes you powerless and the poor have to struggle to rise above the high costs of living on your own. When a group comes together it divides the burdens and costs. It also undermines the capitalist systems method of keeping people in poverty. So, then they can break free from that poverty.

Poverty only exists in a society that forces its monetary system upon everyone and where the rich class and middle class control all the resources. That's corruption. If people have access to their own way to produce food, water, clothing, shelter, etc., then they have successfully defeated poverty without any monetary support. And most other things they do not need in the first place. I'd rather have people drop out from school and not go to college to join me and help invest in my temple being set up like a commune. This will truly help people more than college will.

It will truly help the people because we have to start somewhere and sometime. We have to start at the bottom and we have to start now. True change for the better for the people will never come from the top down first. Change has to come from the bottom up. We have to start now and that means people have to make a sacrifice for the good of the whole community, our commune, our temple. We can no longer just think of ourselves in a selfish, greedy, mercenary fashion. This only breeds the type of people the rich class need to maintain control over their poverty slave class or the worker class. We have to be concerned about our environment, our health, our future, and our present. We have to stop conforming to a system that is destroying the world and oppressing the people. We have to begin to unite for a greater cause than ourselves. I am here to help those that will

help me on my quest for Spiritual Evolution on our path toward Divine Human Utopia, glimmering with the enchantment of Sacred Freedom and Egalitarian Self-Government.

Socialist Escorts Part 1

My idea of Socialist Escorts stems from several beliefs. First is my spiritual religious belief in the concept of the Holy Whore. Briefly, this is symbolic of a Priest or Priestess that represents the god/goddess and through worship and reenactment of the divine copulation fulfilling the desires of others who represent also the corresponding god/goddess often being the opposite sex, but is perfectly fine with same-sex partners and divine aspects as well. Second, as a Socialist trying to break free from the capitalist enslavement poor people cannot afford the sexual fulfillment they need to be healthy human beings. In a Socialist system or more accurately a Communist system we eliminate the money itself that is the method for creating the classes of enslavement. The sacred and honorable job/career of the Holy Whore carries over in the Socialist system as well as any human system. In a capitalist system mainly those with the economic power can afford the escorts they need, while many poverty slaves go unfulfilled. In the Socialist system everyone does their job and is rewarded for this service to their society through the benefits they receive in return. Thirdly, based upon the Social Sexual Psychology of my temple Sex is not just a desire, but a human need that must be fulfilled regularly in order for humans to be healthy both physically and mentally. Without such fulfillment sexual repression manifests in many forms of natural mental and physical conditions such as depression, insomnia, weakened immune systems leading to physical illnesses, etc.

Socialist Escorts Part 2

Escorts in the west are charging insanely high prices for their services. This is based upon a combination of high prices from inflation, the high cost of living, and pure greed. We will offer lowered priced services to External Members and cost less (free in a sense) services to our Internal Members that have chosen to give up the form of wealth of the capitalist world and the money that creates classes which enslaves us. Wealth comes in many forms besides what we are familiar with in the capitalist system. Wealth is having all of our needs provided for by our own people and work and maintained continuously. Wealth can be the ability and leisure to pursue our Artistic Endeavors. Wealth can be the privileged right of the ambiance of luxurious and exotic travel. Through our Socialist Escorts we can create a new world of Spiritual Wealth for our people.

The Basic Unifying Principles of the Church of the Antichrist 999

The church of Satan and Laveyan unifying principle if it can be called that is based around self-godhood, mercenary wealth, power, and mainly atheism. The so-called brotherhood of Satan unifying principle is a belief in the actual christian Satan and supposedly a real brotherhood or family like mentality. The so-called joy of Satan unifying principle is also a belief in the actual christian Satan but with a focus on white power and neo-nazi beliefs. All of these groups and most others have similar unifying principles. The unifying principle of the Church of the Antichrist 999 is a belief in the Antichrist 999 concept.

This is not the direct Antichrist Concept from the christian new testament but borrowing some aspects for spirituality, reference, and imagery. Our Antichrist concept represents an Avatar of Satanic Creation which is symbolized in an actual Satanic Leader and all of those who support the concept of the Antichrist 999. All therefore represent and symbolize the Antichrist together and therefore become Antichrists as well. All other organizations which do not recognize the Antichrist concept and work against the Church of the Antichrist 999 with counter beliefs and goals are seen as organizations created by false prophets. The chosen Prophet, Messenger, Apostle, High Priest, and Avatar of the Church of the Antichrist 999 is the one and only Rev. Caesar 999.

Our unifying principles also include true spirituality and sacred sexual worship given to Satanic Creation, Kali, other Deities, the Prince Beast 999 or Antichrist 999 Avatar aka High Priest, The Whore of Babylon or chosen High Priestess, all Priests, Priestesses, and Members, etc. Therefore, Sexual Fulfillment is one of the major unifying principles within the Church of the Antichrist 999 and the newer Satanic Kali Temple of Kama. This Sexual Fulfillment is temple based with a focus on Tantra, Courtesans, Escorts, Priest/ess Centered, Devadasis, Holy Whores, Orgia, etc.

The next major unifying focus is on our New Age form of Socialist Communalism where equality is an essential part of our temple and everyone does their part or job in return for all the benefits necessary for mental and physical health and spiritual-material prosperity. This is symbolized through interdependence rather than a total mercenary independent system which capitalism perpetuates with its class base poverty slavery. This is in stark contrast to most Satanic Groups like Laveyans, etc. who do not have any real spiritual foundation and represent more of an anti-religion than a real and true spiritual religion. So, the Church of the Antichrist 999 is more of a Socialist based organization which is polytheistic, monotheistic, and pantheistic at the same time. We also have a focus upon matriarchal religion, especially within our Satanic Kali Temple of Kama!

A Short Description of What We Expect From Our Satanic Priests and Priestesses

A Satanic Priest/ess of my Church of the Antichrist 999 and Satanic Kali Temple of Kama must be loyal to my Temple/Church and to me as the High Priest. Our Satanic Priests must follow our Anti-christian or Satanic Moral-Value System, be a Warrior, and or a Holy Whore, be supportive of Gay Rights, support Polygamy, Escorting, Prostitution, Pandering, they must Recruit, requires some Self-Sacrifice, some Ego Denial, and Teach these Satanic Values and Views to our people, they must support our New Age form of Socialism or Communalism based upon interdependence and not total independence, etc. The job of the Satanic Priest/ess in our Church/Temple is to spiritually fight and go to war against the moral cops/soldiers of the right-hand path that work to maintain the judeo-christian moral-value system and its laws! This includes people of the left-hand path that still cling to what we believe to be and have classified as right-wing or judeo-christian values. We see this as a Spiritual War of opposing moral-value systems.

Satanic Buddhists Advanced

Satanic Buddhism is a combination of advanced spiritual principles and our unique form of Satanism that embraces specific religious, carnal, and philosophical ideals that creates a new type of medium level spiritual human being. This new type of medium level spiritual human being transcends from complete and total carnal and material selfishness and unites with their Spiritual Self and Creation as one. Therefore, combining both aspects into one path much like many ancient Buddhist Sects followed embracing Sexual Yoga and Sexual Tantra, etc.

This path leads us to less selfishness and more devotion to fulfillment of the whole community. This addresses the need for people to take on job roles necessary to help fulfill the needs and desires of the whole community. So, it becomes apparent that job roles beyond meditation, yoga, and tantra, etc., need to be filled through self-sacrifice for the good of the community rather than just the self alone.

The advanced Buddhist recognizes that we must move beyond greed and selfishness and therefore a need for accumulating money. So, the need for personal money becomes unnecessary and they carry out whatever job responsibility they are capable of performing that is necessary to fulfill the needs and desires of the whole community.

Tax the Rich

Currently there are about 300 million people in the U.S. Out of that 300 million there are only about 3 million millionaires and about 400 billionaires. There are supposedly about 135 million people in the middle class. This leaves about 162 million people in extreme poverty slavery! I believe the numbers are much higher! The rich class created capitalism, the money, classes, and the oppression of poverty slavery. They are the absolute source and cause of all suffering of the people from financial enslavement. There should be no taxes in the first place and no tax forced upon a people already forced into poverty slavery. If there must be a tax, then there must only be a tax on the rich class who are oppressive rulers of their capitalist empires. I propose a 10% tithe or tax placed upon the rich class! This tax would immediately amount to about $340 billion dollars to be used 100% to help the poverty slaves who suffer the most. This money must be used to create state jobs for the poor, with paid training, rent free housing, free transportation, free work clothing, free food, etc. The rich class has been making us suffer for far too long and it's time for them to start paying up their dues back to the people! If they don't submit to our demands we will gather 162 million people on their capital and shutdown the government!

The End of Money Equals the End of Poverty

Money can be used temporarily against the capitalists and rich class by building socialistic like systems that enable the people to break free of needing money and living life without money. People must stop being brain washed and conditioned into the for profit and gain mentality. We must teach the youth to do work for their people and not just for themselves and not for profit. In return all things necessary for human health mentally and physically are provided. So, the goal is to eliminate money and this will eliminate the class system and ultimately poverty. The end of money equals the end of poverty!

The End of Money Part 2

The money was created by the elitist aristocracy to secure their power and as a tool to enslave us. It seems like a good invention because it allows for an easier exchange when barter is not possible or reasonable. What it does though is create poverty slavery by establishing a class system based upon a monetary standard instead of gold, etc., which moves them away from the more complex aristocracy, royalty, etc., and an overt rule by force method. So, now it's more covert, passive aggressive, so-called democratic, etc.

People are cast down instantly into the poverty slave class when they have no wealth and given a slim chance to rise from total destitution to a slightly more luxurious lifestyle. The majority will never rise above the poverty slave class or the whole system comes crashing down for the rich elitists. So, all their claims to end poverty are bold lies and deception. Poverty will exist until the money is destroyed and the elitists along with it.

What happens is that people knowing no other way out of their situation embrace the take care of your own philosophy which is logical but this only perpetuates the problem as I was saying. For example, we try to build businesses, to make money to escape the burdens placed upon us by the rich class by creating the money and classes. Do not forget they purposely created this poverty and suffering! The full burdens like all the bills, etc., from being taught to be totally independent enable them to keep you down for as long as possible without quickly escaping poverty slavery. They don't want you to cut the burdens down or in half, because it means they have less power over you and less power means they have to spend more money (more power) to control you and manipulate you (go to work, pay bills, buy necessities, etc.). To the rich, we are considered the slave workers to be exploited as cheaply as possible. They look at the entire working force as a market of people to be bought as cheaply as possible to produce their products and increase their wealth from the working power of the people. So, we are nothing to them but servants that they buy up in the market of people (worker slaves to them).

Without Socialist Organization there would be no unions to make job conditions better, no disability, no social security, no benefits, etc. Every little thing has had to be fought for and when the people finally get the numbers up to be able to actually vote them out like they did in the 50's in the u.s., then the rich elitists attack the people and make laws against them, arrest them, torture them, destroy their lives, execute them, etc. This was known as McCarthyism. The McCarthy anti-communist scum served the rich class as they led an open war on the people who fought back with the glory of Communism!

My point is that eventually we will have to make more people realize that business and self-interests are not going to free us from the burdens of capitalism and never free us from poverty alone. What I teach is how we can use our Temple and Businesses to develop Socialist like systems that will truly free us from the burdens of capitalism and poverty slavery!

Kali Temple

In my polytheistic and pantheistic belief system I accept all deities except the abrahamic god which I deny and oppose. As you know it's the god of christians, jews, and muslims. My current beliefs are still eclectic and self-designed but I favor different aspects of Hinduism and their Pantheon. The main deity of my Tantric Hindu Temple is Kali. I'm adopting much of the Shakti Hindu Tradition which is very Matriarchal.

Holy Whore Priest/ess

Our religion of Spiritual Satanism 999 and its parallel of Tantric Hinduism teaches us the beauty and glory of becoming a Holy Whore in service to our People and Satanic Creation, Kali, Shiva, etc. We teach that the Holy Whore Priest/ess is a highly respectable, honorable, dignified, and beautiful profession! We must spread the beauty and power of the Holy Whoredom! Those Women who oppose the Holy Whore represent judeo-christian and feminist values which we strongly must fight against. Our Anti-christian or Satanic Moral-Value System supports the natural beauty of sexuality and its spiritually divine nature!

The World of Devadasi

There are many ideas and beliefs I want to convey. In this article I want to reveal some of the lingering right-hand path and right-wing conservative values that are still being inculcated today, even in the more liberal youth. This is also being carried on within left-hand path and left-wing liberal groups. I teach that anti-Promiscuity, anti-Whoredom, anti-Prostitution, anti-Polygamy, anti-Homosexuality, and several other values and lifestyles connected with specific sexual institutions and cultural developments are mainly associated with and have their origins in more right-hand path and right-wing conservative valued cultures and religions.

This means that I am saying these value related practices and lifestyles are mainly condemned by judeo-christian dominated cultures and did not exist as extensively before their existence. We are more concerned with the modern world than the ancient and we have been experiencing the inculcation of the judeo-christian moral-value system in the west for several thousand years now. This has also contaminated much of the world's cultures and religions making them more fanatical and conservative within their value systems. This has been especially true with Hinduism, etc. We have seen Hindus under the pressure of christians to become what they call more "civilized" and less degenerate in their values.

The Erotic Sexually based civilizations of India and much of Asia were already in decline with the rise and spread of islam, and then christianity became heavily entrenched in India and work to inculcate their values to this day. The war of opposing moral-value systems is very ancient along with the war between Matriarchal and Patriarchal religious systems which also effect political/economic structures.

In many parts of the world different religions especially Matriarchal ones had sacred sexuality and the Holy Whoredom with its Priestesses. Men's desires were fulfilled when necessary and donations went into the Temples. The Priestesses lived with great honor, respect, wealth, and glory around the world! Where Patriarchal religions began to clash with Matriarchal ones wars would take place and where the Patriarchal systems prevailed the Matriarchal systems were merged together and so in many places like India the ancient Holy Whores continued on, but under Priestly Brahman dominion. They still carried on the old ways and lived very glorious and wealthy lives. This is not to say there was no negative exploitation, but this is to be expected on some level when you have a wealthy class dominating everything.

When you believe in the Tantric Universal Creation and how the Goddess Kali manifested itself into 2 parts one becoming Kali and the other Shiva and they unite together in divine sexual union, as all of creation is born into existence, you begin to understand why sexuality and sexual fulfillment is beautiful and important. So, it becomes the duty of the Holy Whore Priestess to become Kali and take on her role and fulfill all the men she can who represent Shiva. This is done in absolute worship and

devotion to Shiva and Kali, etc.! This is much like how many other cultures and deities were worshipped as well.

Everyone takes care of everyone in the community, united by the Temple and the Goddess and God of Creation which are ultimately one and Kali-Yellamma as the Supreme Brahman. This is a very Socialistic Communal lifestyle and all are rewarded and benefited. The Priestesses also learn many other arts and practices including traditional Indian Dance, Singing, and Musical Instruments, etc.

The world of Devadasi existed in a mainstream society for hundreds of years spread across much of Asia! It lasted for centuries even after its decline. Only in the last 50 years has it begun to degrade into simple prostitution which we highly support by itself but look with disdain upon the religious cultural disintegration of such a beautiful and ideal Satanic Culture as we would classify it.

The fanatical right-wing Hindus with their new age agenda pushed on by right-wing christian feminists and priests who wish to transform the Indian values into their own have created laws which strip the Devadasi from the Temples and this has caused the direct loss of all the traditional skills they were taught for generations to survive. Now, the Brahman Priests managed to first have the traditional erotic dancing taught to their wives and daughters. This is basically a method of stealing arts from a group of people they classified as a much lower caste and were working to eliminate the caste altogether. They then stripped out much of the eroticism in the dancing making it more conservative, along with more conservative outfits which reveal hardly any body parts. Most ancient Indian women went topless as nudity and sexuality was not so looked down upon in those times.

We are seeing the last remains of an ancient world built around what we would term as Satanic Eroticism from our rebellious awakening from judeo-christian fanaticism and cultural stagnation. There were similar worlds across the planet and they resonate with our modern ideals and values which I classify as anti-christian or Satanic. So, from our Satanic Moral-Value System we see the Devadasi Culture as a parallel to the modern Satanic Eroticism which we work to build as we undermine the judeo-christian moral-value system in the west.

Now, I get to the heart of this discussion about modern values in the west. The western youth are still being inculcated with what I classify as a judeo-christian value that opposes sexual promiscuity. They purposely guard the secret of the ancient Holy Whore from the youth and so they have no idea of its true beauty and glory which was held on high in ancient times far above the pathetic christian christ. We work to cast down their putrid pure image of their christ and replace him with the Holy Whore once again! The great lover of many will be restored and glorified! Hail the Holy Whore!

The young women today have already begun to walk down the road of the Holy Whore but still they are very selective in their sexual encounters. This is more of an ego issue, but it's still relevant. The western youth are also inculcated with a selfish mercenary

philosophy which is the base of the capitalist system and helps the rich class maintain their diabolic power over the masses. The Devadasi and all Priest/esses that truly believe in their Deities of Creation and who are truly Spiritual know that surrendering their ego is necessary for true worship and devotion. Self-sacrifice is all important for community and the good of the whole people of the Temple.

During the height of the Hippy counter-cultural movement Free Love was a powerful liberal movement but even their sexual activities were still far more selective than is necessary for the true Holy Whore Priestess or Devadasi to achieve their goal in worship and devotion. Therefore, we represent Free Love times 10 and the resurrection of the Holy Whore in a New Age Super Sexual Revolution! We promote promiscuity and the Holy Whore to the youth and our people! We wish for them to give their bodies to Kali/Shiva or what we call Satanic Creation and ultimately to all our people in divine Satanic Eroticism! Join our symbolic Church of the Antichrist 999 and our Satanic Kali Temple of Kama and help us to completely undermine and overturn the judeo-christian moral-value system throughout the world! Deny the christian christ and hail the Holy Whore!

The Sexual Science of Mind and Body

This is only an introduction to my Sexual Science of Body and Mind.

I teach that psychology, behavioral psychology is based upon lies and deception for the purpose of making money and control. These psychologists, psychiatrists, and the drug companies make billions of dollars per year. These organizations and people are murderers, killing millions of people every single year in the name of profit and careers! Psychology is nothing more than a form of mysticism, backed and sponsored by their government partner. I would support other forms of mysticism like Scientology and my own Sexual Science of Mind and Body before I would ever support psychology.

I first called my science Sexual Psychology but I'm not happy with that terminology. The basics of this Sexual Science declares that there is no such thing as anything abnormal. This completely shatters the theories, ideas, and methods of psychologists and psychiatrists who work from a ground zero point of view that there is a state of being normal. This ground zero point of view ultimately leaves open the door to allowing the practitioner to plant or inculcate their religious and social moral-values into their screening and diagnosis methods which ultimately contaminates the entire process and conclusion based upon theoretical mental diseases which they simply invented and are make-believe.

Once we establish this foundation that there is nothing abnormal we can begin to truly see what is normal and natural, including human nature. Ultimately, everything that humans do is normal. There is not a hidden disease of mind that makes us abnormal. There are only natural symptoms of our normal experiences and reactions. Some of these are negative and cause problems or disturbances, but none are abnormal. It is even human nature to try to classify others as abnormal as our natural social screening process helps us maintain the world we feel most comfortable within or what we simply are used to understanding or being part of in a sense.

The business of psychology will eventually be completely annihilated and their partnership with government totally destroyed when enough people awaken to this reality and deny their false services, their drugs, and their lies! This will also probably be when capitalism is crushed world-wide and the rich class finally face their crimes against humanity and the world!

The Cultural Pyramid

1. The Elite Imperial Knights aka Warrior-Priests naturally dominate through Strength, Discipline, Spirituality, and Honor. They make the greatest sacrifice for their people through constant training and development of their bodies and minds. They practice many martial arts, and healing arts, etc. This order allows both men and women, but may have branches of a single sex.

2. The Holy Whore Priest/ess serves through the sacred sexual arts fulfilling the desires of those in need. This is also a Spiritual Path. They learn and teach many sacred rituals, and arts. Many of these include sexual healing, tantra, courtesan, musical instruments, singing, dancing, healing arts, etc.

3. The People's Militia serves part-time through providing extra defense in time of need. They spend part of their time training in martial arts and healing arts, etc. The rest of their time they spend on more personal matters, or other forms of work.

The Knowledge of Sorcery

The Knowledge of Sorcery is a resource worth millions which can be transferred to a book for safe keeping and to spread to the masses. This knowledge can be direct or coded in symbolism, metaphor, parable, etc. These are my Grimoires and they contain many lessons, principles, and vast amounts of spiritual teachings. Remember, limitations are barriers and to destroy barriers you must eliminate your limitations! To eliminate your limitations you must learn and retain all the knowledge that you can. I offer you the student my teachings both in book form and orally.

I currently offer you my book Satan's Sorcery Volume I which is an introduction to my art of Satanic Sorcery as a combination book with my book The Satanic Bible. You can get both of these books in one book for a lower price than book stores from me directly. If you are interested contact me by replying or sending an email to me.

drcaesar999@gmail.com or ghpublish@gmail.com

The Prerequisite Rules for Membership and Priest or Priestess Approval

1. Must be anti-christian (anti-judeo-christian-islamic/anti-the abrahamic god).
2. Must be Socialist, Communist, Communalist, or our New Age Socialist, etc.
3. Must be anti-capitalist (anti-the rich class and upper middle class, anti-large corporations, anti-money, etc.).
4. Must be anti-Laveyan (church of Satan group).
5. Must be bisexual, gay, lesbian, or support full gay rights!
6. Must believe theistically in our Satanic Creation (not the christian concept of Satan, devil, or evil), Kali, or Shiva, etc.
7. Must swear allegiance to First Priest/High Priest Caesar 999, the Church of the Antichrist 999, and the Satanic Kali Temple of Kama.
8. Must recognize the main doctrines of Spiritual Satanism 999 and Tantric Hinduism contained within Rev. Caesar's Satanic Bible and his other spiritual books.
9. Must be anti-conservative feminist.
10. Must be anti-joy of Satan (joy of Satan group).
11. Must be anti-brotherhood of Satan (brotherhood of Satan group).
12. Must be anti-order of the black cathedral (order of the black cathedral group).
13. Must be anti-Luciferian (The Order of Phosphorus and The Church of Adversarial Light groups). (Note: This list is current June 2011.)

Allegiance and loyalty is important. Members of other groups are loyal to them and their selves. This means they will work to benefit their groups and themselves. This is a matter of competition and the dominion of our own cult and power. Oaths are a serious matter. We may never know if they do, but the idea is to keep people in check and make sure they are not openly denying our beliefs and goals. That is only a short list by the way. There are degrees of membership in any group. Those who wish to advance to higher internal degrees will subject themselves to background checks, etc. This list is meant to help simplify things from the beginning and keep out those we already know are counter-productive to our beliefs and goals. Members may be friends with other groups and have affiliations, but they do at their own risk. Some groups may become allies in the future or those not listed already may be considered potential allies.

A Working Class Hero Essay

Some people are brainwashed into believing it's a great thing to have a job and work for some rich company. They see being unemployed as being a bum and that one should work to support themselves. This kind of thinking is disturbing and backward. It is not a great thing to work or to have a job, because it simply means that you are a slave serving a master in the capitalist system for meager wages which will barely cover the costs of living which are tied into the capitalist system.

Nature does not make us slaves for money, only people do. In Nature we only must find food, water, shelter, clothing, and companionship. Organized civilization under the dominion of various cult powers and belief systems create organized slavery which departs from nature's intention of basic survival. This is done under the guise of becoming more spiritual or civilized when in reality they are using a diabolical scheme to keep an elitist group in control of everything. We do know that human greed and possessive nature is a major cause of most problems and this gives gangs of educated and wealthy thugs more ability to control out of the fear of total disintegration of order and safety.

Self-serving and family serving is a basic instinct which Nature or Creation has provided for us. This has led to higher degrees of corrupt civilization especially within capitalism under the elitist rich class. Family Serving is the key to great spiritual civilization. This is not the family unit of christianity, but the family of a tribe or society. A free person should not be subject to a society or civilization they do not believe in or its form of monetary control and trade. This free person should also not be subject to the ideals of those people and mocked or shamed with such degrading insults such as being called a bum.

When the rich class created the capitalist system they designed it to be corrupt from the beginning, to maintain the rich class forever, to maintain a majority of poverty slaves, and never to have enough jobs for every citizen. So, you're always going to have thousands of so-called bums especially when they start manipulating the economic system to purposely cause it to crash and so people perceive it as a depression or recession. People also have the right to not conform with the system and so there will always be those who live on the streets or collect welfare that could find jobs but most will find it hard or impossible to find a job.

The people who complain about others on welfare and having to pay taxes into it should be asking the rich class why they should have to be paying taxes at all? There should be 1,000 times more welfare and greater benefits for all! There also should be enough jobs for everyone and free housing, medical, etc. The elitist rich class instead wants to maintain the most wealth that they can and make us all suffer and serve. The rich class wants an iron grip on power, wealth, resources, and population.

So, instead of calling someone a bum, you should be saying look at that free person, look a refugee! Do not judge people based upon whether they have a job or not unless they chose to be part of a society that requires them to work for honor, otherwise they don't deserve such degradation. People are so stuck up with their standards and want to rid their area of what they see as annoying homeless people that are obviously broke, jobless, have no help, or choose to live this way. The other problem I admit is that these areas breed more criminal activity but some of that activity is not true criminal activity but that's for another discussion.

The criminals are at the top of the food chain as well as at the bottom, that's what I say about that. People should be free from being enslaved by a specific society, but have some where to turn to or a safe haven away from the dangers of the streets created by those on the top in the first place. Out of the chaos comes street gangs who battle with each other and the official rulers. No other civilization in history would have allowed street gang thugs to exist side by side with the official ruling order unless they served a purpose to keep them around.

One has to ask what purpose does street gangs and thugs serve to society and the official ruling order? The answer is quite simple they provide a necessary level of crime to keep a corrupt official order maintaining a specific level of income or financing, higher level of employment rates for their own political, religious, or race, and back door underground mafia style capitalism. Therefore, to eliminate all the problems would be far less profitable! The same thing occurs with the military. If they create true peace and stop all wars then it would be far less profitable! This is what capitalism creates, the ultimate world-wide corruption. In the capitalist system everything is a racket, the law and order racket, the military racket, the economic/political racket, the health care racket, the religious racket, the banking racket, etc.

So, knowing all this corruption exists and it's built into the capitalist system, one has to also ask like the late John Lennon did, "A Working Class Hero is something to be?" There are no bums, only slaves and refugees! In the capitalist system we are forced to be self-serving but we have a choice to try to create a new society where we can serve that society instead of the rich class in order to help ourselves and family only. We can be honored for serving our true family and people in a truly egalitarian society. Everyone else can choose to remain forever in the jungle of the capitalist system as a slave or refugee!

Kali Manifest

I draw upon and summon the dark force of Kali, Mother Vampress! We are one being from which I draw strength and power from her blood, the Life Force of Creation. Goddess Kali, is life, death, and the undead! We are the eternal spirit and eternal body. I shall reincarnate eternally! I am immortal through your power oh great Dark Mother Kali!

Allegiance and Loyalty

Allegiance and loyalty is important. Members of other groups are loyal to them and their selves. This means they will work to benefit their groups and themselves. This is a matter of competition and the dominion of our own cult and power. Oaths are a serious matter. We may never know if they do, but the idea is to keep people in check and make sure they are not openly denying our beliefs and goals. That is only a short list by the way (See: The Prerequisite Rules for Membership and Priest or Priestess Approval). There are degrees of membership in any group. Those who wish to advance to higher internal degrees will subject themselves to background checks, etc. This list is meant to help simplify things from the beginning and keep out those we already know are counter-productive to our beliefs and goals. Members may be friends with other groups and have affiliations, but they do at their own risk. Some groups may become allies in the future or those not listed already may be considered potential allies.

Staircase of Ascension

Life is a staircase of ascension. We must take one step at a time. Sometimes we fall back a few steps but that is the fate of every staircase and everyone which ultimately is linked together, one affects the other. Your mistakes affect you and others. So, everything is but a step upon the grand staircase toward the ultimate reward. When you reach the top, the glory will fill your spirit. Then another staircase is presented to you as you begin again.

What Satanic Kali Represents

Satanic Kali is the Great Holy Whore. She represents divine sexuality, sexual fulfillment, erotica, promiscuousness, orgies, homosexuality, bisexuality, polygamy, polyandry, sexual tantra, sexual yoga, erotic classical Indian dance, classical Indian music, courtesan, Devadasi Priestess and Priest, Shakti, matriarchy, sexual energy, kundalini, vampirism, blood, life-force, immortality, spiritual alchemy, meditation, healing arts, sexual healing, magick, sorcery, craft making, etc.

Mass Boycott and Traditional Roles

We would like to emphasize some traditional roles for our new society which also help to break us free from the capitalist system which undermines us and makes us poverty slaves. For example we need to resurrect and maintain our craft skills before they are completely lost! Capitalist upper class controlled machines must not replace traditional human ingenuity in the form of craft skills, etc.! Technology is being used against humanity in the name of profit! When technology is used to undermine the lowest class of workers and rob them of their independent and interdependent village abilities to live without being completely subject to the slave system of capitalism and forced into their sweat shops for meager wages then that technology along with those employing it have become the enemy of these people if not already. It becomes necessary for a mass boycott of such products produced upon those machines in order to cause the collapse of those companies and a restoration of traditional craft workers way of life or the total separation from that class enslavement under the capitalist rich class and upper middle class. We support the mass boycott of products produced upon machines made by rich and upper middle class corporations, etc. We would like to see Woman take on more traditional roles of the Pleasure-r and Holy Whore for Men to help keep up their morale, the role of Child Barer, the role of House and Temple Priestess, the role of Craft Maker, etc. We would like Men to embrace some traditional roles as well, the role of the Warrior-Priest, Craft Worker, Craft Skills Expert, etc. Some of these roles are pre-christian in origin, what they would call Pagan! These roles are not considered to be concrete, just important to emphasize but being a truly liberal group we are open to what is viewed as more modern roles. Some of the modern roles today were accepted in ancient pre-christian times. Some of these roles you may not understand, since judeo-christian values still dominate modern society even during this time of judeo-christian decline. We however work to supersede those values with our semi-new system combined with many ancient pre-christian moral-values and views.

The Pagan Empire

Terms like gay, lesbian, straight, heterosexual, homosexual, bisexual, etc. were either used or created by jew and christian psychologists trying to define what is a normal and abnormal personality based upon their religious moral-values. Therefore, they tried to use the false science of psychology to establish and raise up their judeo-christian moral-value system along with reinforcing civil laws which outlaw practices they defined as abnormal and immoral. As an anti-christian it is my duty to undermine and establish anti-christian moral-values and moral view points. This must also be the duty of all anti-christians and when we say anti-christian this also means anti-judaist and anti-muslim, etc. The christian morals are just an extension of the disgusting jew values and muslims cling to very similar values but some differ. So, when we refer to the oppositional values, we simply say the judeo-christian moral-value system. What I have seen and realized is that what it all comes down to is a war of opposing moral-value systems. Therefore, we work to undermine the judeo-christian moral-value system and work toward its ultimate destruction on earth as a majority system. As the Anti-christ Power we symbolically cast down the judeo-christian moral-value system and work to raise up those values, views, and lifestyles that have been condemned, looked down upon, outlawed, outcast, etc. I've tried to define many of these counter-values and views which are all our rights to practice. Here I will again try to list some of these anti-christian moral-values and views. These are all supported by our anti-christian or Satanic Moral-Value System which is the major doctrine in my Satanic Bible. What we support is Homosexuality, Bisexuality, Gay Rights, Gay Marriage and Open Gay Military Service, Polygamy, Polyandry, Prostitution, Pandering, Promiscuousness, Orgies, Sexual Freedom, Teen Sex, Teen Adulthood, Lowered Drinking Age, etc. All those who oppose a single one of these values, views, and rights are our enemies! These practices are what we fight for and raise an army to defend against the judeo-christian forces on earth! All of these practices are condemned within the traditional moral-values of judeo-christians and are pre-christian in origin or Pagan as defined under denigrating christian terms. None of these practices were condemned before the judeo-christian moral and physical invasion infestation of Europe. As we cast off the judeo-christian chains we shall restore each of these pre-christian practices to their former glory. The judeo-christian values seem to linger on in many families despite their separation from church activities. This was noted in the Nazi Religion as they broke away from judeo-christian beliefs and values to re-establish former Pagan beliefs many Germans clinged to judeo-christian values. This clinging nature will slowly disappear once judeo-christians are removed from positions of authority and control. We will restore pre-christian Pagan values to a majority of the world, especially Europe and the U.S. who will become one Empire in the future! This new Empire will be The Pagan Empire!

Shakti Tantric Devotional Worship

My doctrines of Spiritual Satanism 999 describes our Creation Deity as a Universal Consciousness which is the Supreme Feminine Power and she Creates Masculine Energy from herself. This ultimately allows for the worship of almost any God or Goddess which she/he can represent. However, we deny and oppose the abrahamic god and belief systems based upon their dogma, oppressive doctrines, and laws. I have personally chosen Kali or she has chosen me as the main representative deity of our left-hand Shakti Tantric Beliefs.

5 Basic Points of Spiritual Satanism 999

Let's once again define a few points about our religion of Spiritual Satanism 999. 1. It is a unique new religion founded in 1999 by Rev. Caesar 999. 2. It is anti-Laveyan. 3. It is anti-judeo-christian. 4. It is anti-christian Satan in the sense of believing in the christian concept of Satan or devil as a real being and representing evil. 5. It is truly Spiritual and Theistic.

Satan's Divine Vampir Temple

This is the original Satanic Vampir Temple known as Satan's Divine Vampir Temple. All others who claim they started years before will have to show physical proof that they existed before our underground formation. We consider all other cults to be our enemies and we refuse to recognize or associate with them. We focus on Spiritual Alchemy, Transformation of The Self, Development of Unity and The Supreme One, Doctrine of 999, Immortality, Spiritual and Carnal Development, Black Arts, Black Magick, or Satanic Sorcery, etc.

Letter Explaining Some Difference with Laveyan Satanism

Yes, I'm the author and it is completely different. I'm anti-Laveyan. I can give you some brief differences but my religion is very spiritual, deep, and complex. Basically, I represent a new age form of Socialism which is interdependent. This is opposed to the Laveyan independent mercenary system which is also the basis of the capitalist system. I also support many rights and values. The Laveyan system is very right-wing politically even though they may claim otherwise. I am more of the far left politically. So, even though Laveyans religiously follow a left-hand path religion they are mostly right-wing economically and politically. Laveyan philosophy seeks to roll back all the advancements that have been made by civil rights and progressive movements. This is more or less the philosophy of Nietzsche, rand, Redbeard, etc. which I highly oppose. I have many doctrines in my religion of Spiritual Satanism 999. The main core of my system revolves around my Anti-christian or Satanic Moral-Value System. What I see going on is a war of opposing moral-value systems between those of the judeo-christian forces and those who oppose them like myself, etc. My concept of a deity is that of Creation or an Adversarial (Satanic) Creation because Creation is its own adversary. This I see as a Universal Consciousness and we are all part of it as lesser deities but one. This Creation is polytheistic and pantheistic and has both masculine and feminine aspects. So, symbolically this Creation can represent any deity or deities except for the judeo-christian abrahamic god which we deny and oppose. I personally like the Hindu Pantheon and have adopt Kali Shakti system for the main deity of my religion and refer to her as Satanic Kali since we have equated her to our Satanic System. This is the extreme basics. You can purchase my Satanic Bible, my other books, and read my many posts in group/page discussions for more information.

Worship The Holy Whore Priestess and The Holy Whore Priest

As a Spiritual Warrior-Priest I train my inner and outer self to improve myself, defend our true people, and enter a deep mystical spiritual path of Magick and Alchemy. As a Holy Whore Priest I will fulfill the sexual desires of our people who are both men and women who join us and are in need of my sexual healing, etc.! Join us now and become a either a Warrior-Priest, Holy Whore Priestess, or both! As a Holy Whore Priestess you too will fulfill the sexual desires of our people and you will be worshiped in return, given status, spiritual and material wealth, and authority in our temples! We will journey into the mind and body taking us into the systems of Spiritual Satanism 999, Tantrism, Shakti Hinduism, Buddhism, Taoism, etc. We will learn many arts from meditation, yoga, tantra, self-healing, sexual healing, magick, alchemy, to martial arts, etc. The new anti-christian or Satanic Moral-Value System which is the heart of Spiritual Satanism 999 helps us to raise up the Holy Whore once again. Many eastern arts and practices once were widespread and mainstream before more conservative and restrictive systems and beliefs began to force these arts underground. We work to restore the Devadasi, Left-Hand Tantrism, Buddhist Sexual Tantra or Yoga, Taoist Sex Magick, Sexual Healing Arts, Courtesans, etc. The Holy Whore is placed back on a higher level for worship and respect above the average woman/man or conservative minded! The Holy Whore is greater than the woman/man that refuses to give their sexual healing freely to our brothers and sisters. The conservative and monogamous minded woman/man will be spat upon and looked down upon, even outcast in many places! Those that work to maintain such values that glorify the virgin image and purity of nature are declared enemies of our temples since such values are mainly classified as judeo-christian! The Holy Whore rules and the anti-whore is condemned in our temples! This message we spread as we glorify the Holy Whore Priestess and Holy Whore Priest! Come join us and spread your legs for your People and Temples, for Kali, Shiva, and Satanic Creation, etc. Bring your donations to our temples and raise up the Holy Whore Priestess once again. We cast down their christ and resurrect the Holy Whore Priestess!

To Be a Holy Whore

Our religion teaches you to act like a whore, dress like a whore, and to be a whore! This is what we teach is holy! This is the Holy Whore! Those who oppose this are our enemies!

The Holy Whore Priestess was revered around the world through various cultures and religions long before the christian christ! This is not about inverted christianity or blasphemy. This is about true Sexual Spirituality and Satanic Eroticism! (Naturally Adversarial Eroticism)

I was trying to express how this form of sexual union or Tantra involves a highly spiritual connection and ritualistic performances tied to the deity or deities in worship and devotion. The sex is not just for the sake of pleasure itself, but this of course is a secondary aspect. When we embrace a Holy Whore Priestess she represents the Goddess (Kali, etc.) of our Temple and he represents the God (Shiva, etc.). She fulfills his desires through true worship, devotion, and service to the community and deity. This is a sacred and spiritual profession that we must restore to its full glory and honor!

Mystical Satanism

My form of Spiritual Satanism is the only true form of Spiritual Satanism since I don't find other groups to be truly spiritual. I'd also like to define my form of Satanism as Mystical Satanism! Almost every aspect of my beliefs involve deep spiritual mystical symbolism and ritualism which is probably what confuses a lot of people when trying to learn my form of Satanism.

If you're just looking to be selfish and fulfill your own needs and not embrace any form of spirituality and mystical understanding then this form of Satanism is not for you. If you just want to party and listen to metal music then this form of Satanism is not for you. If you do not believe in giving your loyalty and allegiance to a Temple and its founders then this form of Satanism is not for you. If you are anti-religion and just want to live by a philosophy this form of Satanism is not for you. If you want to worship the actual christian devil or Satan this form of Satanism is not for you. If you consider yourself the highest god and authority this form of Satanism is not for you.

Mystical Satanism or Spiritual Satanism 999 has a deity which is Satanic Creation which is symbolic of all of Creation or the Universe or Universal Consciousness. This can therefore represent almost any form of deity or deities except for the judeo-christian god which we deny and oppose. The judeo-christian and islamic god is one and the same and we are highly focused on opposing their belief systems. Therefore, we represent true anti-christian beliefs, etc. Now, the deity that we recognize the most as representing and symbolizing this Universal Consciousness is the Goddess Kali! She is the Great Dark Mother! From the beginning she symbolizes the Universe and divides herself into her feminine and masculine form through which they unite in a Tantric Sexual Union. This Cosmic Sexual Dance is The Sacred Marriage and so the beauty of Sexual Union as a mystical concept to be worshipped is set up from the very beginning.

She is the Great Holy Whore Mother! All of her followers will embrace the Holy Whore and spread the sacred arts of Tantra, Dance, Healing Arts, and Priestess/Priesthood. When Kali is angered and needs to protect her children her rage is unparalleled and so the Warrior Class is born in her image as the Warrior-Priests and Warrior-Priestesses. You can become a either a Warrior-Priest, Holy Whore Priestess, or both! As a Holy Whore Priestess you too will fulfill the sexual desires of our people and you will be worshiped in return, given status, spiritual and material wealth, and authority in our temples!

We will journey into the mind and body taking us into the systems of Spiritual Satanism 999, Tantrism, Shakti Hinduism, Buddhism, Taoism, etc. We will learn many arts from meditation, yoga, tantra, self-healing, sexual healing, magick, alchemy, to martial arts, etc. The new anti-christian or Satanic Moral-Value System which is the heart of Spiritual Satanism 999 helps us to raise up the Holy Whore once again. Many eastern arts and

practices once were widespread and mainstream before more conservative and restrictive systems and beliefs began to force these arts underground.

We work to restore the Devadasi, Left-Hand Tantrism, Buddhist Sexual Tantra or Yoga, Taoist Sex Magick, Sexual Healing Arts, Courtesans, etc. The Holy Whore is placed back on a higher level for worship and respect above the average woman/man or conservative minded! The Holy Whore is greater than the woman/man that refuses to give their sexual healing freely to our brothers and sisters.

The conservative and monogamous minded woman/man will be spat upon and looked down upon, even outcast in many places! Those that work to maintain such values that glorify the virgin image and purity of nature are declared enemies of our temples since such values are mainly classified as judeo-christian! The Holy Whore rules and the anti-whore is condemned in our temples! This message we spread as we glorify the Holy Whore Priestess and Holy Whore Priest!

Come join us and spread your legs for your People and Temples, for Kali, Shiva, and Satanic Creation, etc. Bring your donations to our temples and raise up the Holy Whore Priestess once again. We cast down their christ and resurrect the Holy Whore Priestess!

Satanic Creation and The Goddess Kali Ma

My form of Theistic Satanism is a branch that does not believe in the christian Satan or their god and we are not atheists! This can be further classified as Spiritual and Mystical Satanism! It is known as Spiritual Satanism 999 to the uninitiated and to the initiated as Vampir Satanism 999. This is the proper spelling of Vampir used for our system! Our concept of a deity or deities is rather a complex concept. We begin with the understanding that it is a Universal Consciousness and represented by all of Creation. This Creation is its own Adversary and therefore can also be called Adversarial Creation or Satanic Creation! Humans are considered lesser deities, yet always one with Creation. This Creation can take on the form of almost any deity and so our forms of worship can be almost endless. However, we deny and oppose the judeo-christian god and it's concept of an evil devil! From this view point we are developing a Pantheon of religious worship and cultures! The main deity chosen for our belief system is the Goddess Kali Ma and therefore reveals the Shakti foundations and development of a Matriarchal System of Tantric Priestess Power with an equally balanced Priesthood! We will refer to Kali sometimes as Satanic Kali to reveal the bridge between our understanding of her role as Supreme Brahman and the Adversarial Nature of Creation!

Rev. Caesar 999's Spiritual Evolution and The Satanic Moral-Value System

When I was in my late teens, I was a Devil Worshiper. Ironically, I couldn't find a single girl into Devil Worshiping or Death Metal, because they simply did not exist in my region at that time! I did meet my best friend who was also a Devil Worshiper, but he was like 1 in a million in my area. So, I was mostly outcast and made fun of by all others including the mainstream Metalheads.

A lot of them were christians or just not religious. My best friend introduced me to Lavey's Satanic Bible and I studied his belief system. What really attracted me most was the call to gather together with like minded individuals and organize a group. So, I was on the Atheistic Laveyan path for awhile. Once again, I still found myself outcast since the same people not only didn't understand the difference but did not care if there was one.

So, my best friend and I had this weird mix of Devil Worshiping and Laveyan Satanism going on but he had no interest in any organized group. So, I began my correspondence with Anton Lavey and talked about organizing my own group. He gave me a piece of advice to buy and study a book on giving speeches. Anyhow, my best friend had died in 97, from a suicide. Also, Lavey had died that same year.

So, once again I was completely alone on my Quest. So, my spiritual evolution continued! I had to completely break free of the judeo-christian belief in a god and their devil, before I could find true spirituality. So, Atheism was not the end of religion for me, but the beginning of a completely new religion! So, my beliefs once again evolved and I developed my own form of Theistic Satanism which is the only true form of Spiritual Satanism, because no other form of Satanism teaches you to think of your people before yourself!

As far as I can tell, all other forms of Satanism fall back on that mercenary selfish and purely individualist mentality which lacks a true spiritual quality! So, I had pulled away from Laveyan Satanism because it lacked true spirituality and truly is a philosophy and not a real traditional religion. I also could not go back to basic Devil Worshiping because I had not only evolved spiritually but intellectually and therefore viewed the simplicity and naivety involved in that form of basic belief system which gives a form of recognition to the existence of the christian god and allows for their continuing enforcement of their dogma mentally and physically.

In this example, a christian priest will tell someone they are sinful and must repent or suffer in hell! Most people brought up on christianity will either repent or revel in the belief they are doing something wrong or against god, based upon the christian dogma that there is only one god and only one true moral-value system. More and more people

today are enlightened and step beyond that frame of mind realizing that is just christian dogma and nonsense.

So, what I do is to help those who simply do not get it yet to become enlightened with the knowledge that they are not immoral! They are only immoral when trapped in the mental cage these christians try to keep them locked inside. Once freed from such dogma, people realize they simply hold an opposing moral view and an opposing moral-value system.

I teach that the core of all religious belief systems are built upon a specific moral-value system. Most of the right hand path religions are built upon a universal system which is most easily described as the judeo-christian moral-value system. So, what I have done is gather from many ancient belief systems, specific values, views, ways of life, that are naturally anti-christian and have been condemned by these right hand religions from the beginning and placed them into my anti-christian or Satanic Moral-Value System, which is the most important core doctrine of my Satanic Religion!

So, what I see has been going on since ancient times is a natural war of opposing moral-value systems and it is therefore our goal to completely overturn the judeo-christian moral-value system! All those who work to maintain the judeo-christian moral-value system are ultimately our enemies!

The Holy Whore Priestess and Sacred Mother

One of the most sacred careers is that of the Holy Whore Priestess! There are Holy Whore Priests as well! This can complement the role as Warrior-Priest or Mother-Wife. The Holy Whore is an ancient concept which existed around the world in many cultures and pre-christian belief systems. One of the main cultures we focus on restoring is that of the Devadasi which is of Indian Culture! We also will focus upon restoring the European Holy Whore which can be found within Greek and Roman Cultures. If anyone knows of a similar culture within other ancient systems of Europe, etc., it would be great to hear about them since most of my research is focused on these main cultures. I see Indian Culture as much of the source of pre-Greek Culture, etc. Also, the Mother-Wife role takes on a spiritual Priestess role as well and a community role. They prepared much of the food, gardening, clothing making, child raising, and spiritual matters in the home itself were generally conducted by the Woman and some public aspects as well. While in ancient times the Man was the Warrior-Priest, Hunter, etc. In pre-christian times we celebrated many festivals, while polygamy and sexual promiscuousness were widespread and considered beautiful and natural! Through Caesar's semi-new or resurrected anti-christian or Satanic Moral-Value System we return to these views and ways of life! So, the Holy Whores great purpose of sexual fulfillment in the name of the God and Goddess is restored! The Tantric foundation is very universal within the Holy Whore Cultures!

I look into the Heavens to view the macrocosm of her cosmic beauty and so shall I see her beauty again, radiant, and reflected in the microcosm of her Earthly Body! She is my High Priestess, The Scarlet Woman, and The Whore of Babylon. I am her High Priest and The Prince Beast 999! Together we unite in the Divine Marriage to fulfill The Great Work! All those that join us will receive the blessing of The Beast and his Sacred Trinity! The Whore of Babylon shall spread her legs and our glory will be reborn!

Mystical Sex Priest

As well as a Warrior-Priest, I am a Mystical Sex Priest. This is also known as the Holy Whore Priest/ess. So it's part of my religion and job to always meditate, think about, talk about, and engage in Tantric Sex and Sexual Meditation. Those who are against these arts and methods are our enemies. I use a Meditation and Tantric Sex Chamber to meditate and think upon my powers and organization. This can't be done properly in a noisy and distracting environment. I favor these arts over the organized rituals others may have an interest in. I was interested more in those kinds of rituals when I was younger, but my Tantric Sex Meditation Art is far more potent and brings the mind to another level. Then all thoughts of knowledge and solutions to questions sought can be found.

Practices of the Holy Whore Priestess

The Holy Whore Priestess or Priest being part of our Goddess of Satanic Creation and out of reverence for our Goddess emulates our Goddess Satanic Kali and her masculine aspect of Satanic Shiva. It is important that the Priestess and Priest learn and understand the basics of the Tantric Creation story which lays the Sexual Foundation of Creation and all things and beings within and without.

Holy Whoredom becomes an important virtue and value within our system and a required practice of our Holy Whore Priestesses and Holy Whore Priests. The Holy Whoredom symbolizes the reenactment of the Holy Union or Divine Marriage of the Masculine and Feminine aspects or Forces of Creation. We establish the sacredness and beauty of these arts and practices, taking place since the beginning of time.

The Holy Devadasi Priestesses embraced many of these practices and arts, becoming the Golden Power of the Temple which became the base of economic abundance, fueling thriving Communities and Great Empires! These ancient Values and Lifestyles can be understood today as more left-hand and middle path value-systems compared to the extreme opposition and dogma of right-hand values-systems at the heart of right-hand path religious systems which have held basically the same views since ancient times.

What we face are right-hand path religious and state authorities who still teach that there is only one true moral-value system which is their own system. There was no other modern organized system to oppose such dogma until now. Today, we bring to you the naturally anti-christian Satanic Moral Value System which is just as authoritative, true, and dignified to us as much as the christian value system is to christians.

We defy the judeo-christian authorities and break through their dark ages of mental conflicts and mental stagnation with this mind expanding epiphany. Arise my Holy Whores and fulfill the desires of our people. Do not be selfish with your bodies and give pleasures to those who need in the name of our Goddess Satanic Kali, in the name of our Church of The Antichrist 999, and Temple of Satanic Kali, all our Sub-Temples, and in the name of The People who need the Powers of Sexual Healing to keep their morale high and build our economic system.

Every Man symbolizes the masculine aspect which we refer to as Satanic Shiva and every Woman symbolizes the feminine aspect Satanic Kali. In this religious theme, Satanic means Adversarial in connection to Creation itself. Creation is its own Adversary. Satanic Creation is seen as a Universal Consciousness and can be represented through any form of deity or deities, except the judeo-christian god which we deny and deeply oppose within our anti-christian or Satanic Religion.

Therefore, we teach and spread the practices expected of our Holy Whore Priestesses. There must be a love of many, promiscuousness, bisexuality, multiple sacred unions, many gifts given to the Holy Whore Priestess and Holy Whore Priest, and this must be known as Sacred, Honorable, Respectable, Dignified, and ultimately Glorified!

The concept of a christ and christian god cast down and the Holy Whore Priestess restored once again to her former glory. The christians tried to cast down the Holy Whore Priestess and replace her with their christ but they have failed and the Holy Whore Priestess will prevail! Rise up now and spread your legs my Holy Whores of Babylon! Rise up my High Priestess, Holy Whore of Babylon! Your High Priest, Prince Beast 999 awaits you! I am the Thunder! You are the Lightning! Here comes the Rain!

Self-Sacrifice and Interdependence

Here we learn several of the major differences between our Satanic Doctrines and the doctrines of our enemies among other Satanic Groups. While other Satanic Groups spread the unspiritual doctrine of selfishness, we highly oppose this doctrine in favor of our truly spiritual doctrine of Self-Sacrifice for the Good of The Whole People and our Temple.

Our bodies do not belong to us. Our bodies belong to our Shakti Goddess, to our Temple, and to our People as an Interdependent Whole. This brings us to another major difference between our Satanic Doctrines and those of other Satanic Groups. While other Satanic Groups teach the unspiritual doctrine of total independent mercenary lifestyles, we teach the spiritual doctrine of Interdependence. It's important for the student of our teachings to understand that just like there are many opposing factions of christianity, there are many opposing factions of Satanic Belief Systems. This form of Satanism is called Spiritual Satanism 999 and it is founded upon aspects of left-hand path and middle path doctrines and values which make it a truly Spiritual Satanic Religion.

Now, we do not ask our supporters and Members to give up their lives completely. We ask that each Member give of themselves at least 10% toward our cause in one form or another. This is in direct proportion to the amount that many jews and christians still give to their churches in the form of a tithe. We must not continue to support selfish mercenary doctrines that will only fill the pockets of those who have only one goal, personal gain and profit. We do not oppose carnal pleasures and some personal gain, but this alone will not build Physical Satanic Temples, will not build a Powerful Organized Priesthood, it will not Repeal jew and christian laws, and it certainly will not Oust jew and christian Rulers from the Seats of Power.

Therefore, it is absolutely necessary to support Spiritual Satanic Doctrines like Self-Sacrifice and Interdependence so that we can make a serious effort to build a serious organized Spiritual Satanic Religion on Earth in Modern Times which will eventually become a New World Religion. I also do not believe this is possible through Satanic Doctrines which symbolize more of a philosophical lifestyle which opposes actual spiritual religion and organized religion itself.

Also, I do not believe it possible through Satanic Doctrines which give acknowledgement of the existence of the judeo-christian god by organizing a religious faith around the christian concept of their devil, no matter if it is represented as good or evil. Our True Brothers and Sisters that give more than 10% toward our cause will be greatly rewarded and honored!

The Pyramid of Honor and Glory

The Pyramid of Honor and Glory begins with the Shakti Goddess Satanic Kali who symbolizes the Supreme Brahman in our system. Satanic Kali is above the Pyramid. She is symbolized by images of Kali, our Satanic Skull and Star surrounded by fire, etc. The top stone is then divided into two parts. The first part of the top stone symbolizes Satanic Kali's feminine aspect in anthropomorphic form which we refer to as the Holy Whore High Priestess 999, Whore of Babylon. The second part of the top stone symbolizes Satanic Kali's masculine aspect known as Satanic Shiva in anthropomorphic form which we refer to in our system as The Antichrist 999 or High Priest Caesar 999, The Prince Beast 999. This is our Satanic Trinity symbolized through 999 which is used for meditation to attain Gnosis or Enlightenment and to become one with Satanic Creation, the Universal Consciousness. The next two stones below the High Priestess and High Priest symbolize to the High Priestesses left side, the Order of The Holy Whore Priestesses and to the right below the High Priest symbolize the Order of the Warrior-Priests. Below them is one long stone which symbolizes The Holy Satanic Army of supporters and followers. Each stone layer in ascending order represents a higher level of Honor, Glory, and Sacrifice to be understood and recognized. Those Women who perform the sacred arts of Holy Whoredom giving their bodies to our Goddess/God, Temple, and People are to be worshiped, honored, and glorified above those who do not. Those Men who perform the sacred arts of the Warrior Priests are to be worshiped, honored, and glorified above those who do not. All those who oppose these arts and full glorification of these arts and the Priestesses and Priests of those arts and the Goddess/God, and Temple are the enemies of the Temple and the People!

More Priest and Priestess Regulations

The Holy Whore Priestess and Warrior-Priest represent the role models of our Satanic Society and Religion. Each Holy Whore Priestess must have at least 5 lovers and they must not all be of perfect desired beauty or desired age. These lovers must be a mix of Men and Women. Each Priestess should practice at least several other arts that will benefit the Temple and People. These other arts could be Classical Indian Dancing, Belly Dance, Massage, Yoga, Tantra, Healing Arts, Courtesan, Singing, etc. All lovers must give gifts to the Temple and Priestesses on the Holy Days. All those who oppose these arts and practices are the enemies of our Church and Temple. All Sub-Temples can have their own High Priest and High Priestess. Any Official Priest or Priestess can form their own Sub-Temple as long as it conforms to the basic beliefs and goals of our main Church and Temple. There can be both male and female Holy Whore Priests as well as male and female Warriors-Priests but some branches may be entirely male or female, according to the rules of the branch.

Capitalist Enemies

I see that often people are confused about the beliefs and goals of my temple. We stand against capitalism, but believe in using capitalism to fight capitalism. We fight fire with fire! We stand against money, the rich class, and the class system in general. These things all create poverty slavery and our goal is to bring an end to poverty slavery. To end poverty slavery the rich class must fall, the class system collapsed, and the money ultimately destroyed. All of these things will happen in time naturally as they become useless to our people through our methods of breaking free. The enemy is not just the judeo-christian, not just the muslim, not just the more fanatical right-hand path religions, but also the rich class and the middle class that supports them. Our method is not a direct political method, but a method of separation through our collective will. I've offered my supporters and followers every opportunity to show their support through work instead of financial support. I've offered low price e-books for those with very little money. I've spent much of my time trying to teach my beliefs freely and often to those not worth my time and those who have wasted my time. I've developed highly spiritual and sophisticated methods of achieving our goals. So, finally I also offer methods which will financially benefit our people and temple as we slowly work toward our higher spiritual goals over time in a more realistic and partly materialistic fashion. This shows our ability and willingness to embrace the carnal and at the same time embrace the spiritual without becoming over fanatical. However, this New Age form of Socialism is not for the masses. Our system is for our people only and everyone else is our enemy. Also, all other satanic groups are our enemies as well. We require our supporters to be 100% loyal to our Church/Temple and they must swear allegiance.

True Communism

So, there are different groups or associations of rich people all vying for power and control, but they work together as a rule when it benefits them and secures their position of power. So, they usually are united under systems that support a class system with a monetary structure. This form of monetary class system structure maintains their wealth and so the rich class associations in one nation, usually support the rich class associations of other nations. Each nation has several associations of rich class that all work against each other on the same and other issues which ultimately benefit those particular associations. These people believe they are aristocracy, royalty, religious crusaders, business men, economic developers, etc. The politics that people see on the surface is more a smokescreen and form of entertainment than some real institution of change and improvement. There is nothing more insincere and degrading to the real people, the masses of poverty slaves, than a bunch of opposing political parties made up of rich class politicians squabbling over how they want to run the nations of the world. Since these people were the ones who originally developed and created these nations that oppress the real people, then it makes sense to deny these nations and let the real people develop their own smaller nations! These must be nations created by the poor class, the poverty slave! These nations must oppose the class system and its monetary base which is what creates the class system in the first place. This is the true reason why Socialist nations have the same problems of capitalist nations, because they maintain the same foundational core of the capitalist systems, which is the monetary base which in turn creates a class system. So, if a Socialist nation has no real intention of becoming a True Communist nation that eliminates the monetary base and class structure, then it will eventually collapse back into a capitalist system of oppression. Therefore, Socialism that does not truly work toward becoming True Communism will ultimately fail and return to capitalism. The Communist system that has a monetary base and class system is not True Communism and it is Socialism which will collapse back into capitalism!

Arm the Youth with Knowledge

The civil war was not a war of freedom, but a war that took away freedom! The civil war proved that we are prisoners of the rich class and their government! If states try to secede from the union and form their own government, they will come under attack by the rich class and their government because they want to control as much territory, people, resources, and wealth as they can. This is the exact same thing that monarchies and dictatorships do with their empires. Most people realize this fact, but are not willing to openly declare this truth! We live in an empire created by the rich class which creates a slave worker class through their monetary system, manipulates the economy, stages terrorist attacks, creates false wars, infects the people with diseases, promotes illegal immigration, and the list goes on and on. The same type of people have been controlling and creating governments for thousands of years. The point of stating these facts is to just make our people aware of the reality of what is truly going on behind the smokescreens. The youth are the most naïve and we will make sure they become aware sooner than they would through their own experience. A youth that is aware, is a youth that is armed against their enemies! We must arm the youth with knowledge, but schools and colleges are not always the answer. This is because governments can control what is taught, public schools teach too little and lack the proper environment, colleges and universities cost too much for the poor. The rich elite of society have long been taught in their schools that they are being taught to run and dominate society. So, they have always had the best and most expensive schools. Schools don't always benefit the people as a whole, when they are designed to prepare people for living completely independent and to solely benefit the self. Meanwhile, the large corporations with millions of dollars are also financed by banks with even more millions because they are looking to make a profit. Banks are controlled by rich people and the government which is also a group of rich people. These banks will not loan money to poor people with no credit and who truly need it. So, the money stays with the rich and they help corporations advance which only undermines the small business with little money. They also undermine the craft worker, by mass producing large quantities of cheaply made products. So, the craft worker is put out of business and they lose their craft skills. Ultimately, rich class owned corporations force millions of poor people or poverty slaves to lose their craft skills and make them slaves to rich class owned corporations which use their machines to mass produce everything. This process is almost 100% complete in the u.s. and has been going on in other countries! Going to their colleges will not restore these craft skills. Our Temple goal is to restore many of these craft skills and work interdependently with our anti-christian or Satanic People.

The Purpose of Member Fees

First of all, our Satanic Religion does not believe in the judeo-christian god or their devil. Also, our Satanic Religion does not believe in the christian antichrist mentioned in their false holy book of revelations. We do not support any doctrine that gives credit to the existence of the christian god and their devil. The term Satanic in our religion is used to symbolize an Adversarial Belief System! This Adversarial Belief System is Adversarial to the judeo-christian religion and god. Also, our Satanic Creation (Universal Consciousness/Satanic Kali) is an Adversarial Creation and is its own Adversary. Our entire belief system is therefore anti-christian based and every member is therefore an Anti-christ! Also, I am the High Priest Prince Beast 999 and Antichrist 999. The christians named the leader and organization of those who will finally defeat them and bring them to their knees. I am this Satanic Leader and Antichrist 999! This is part of a completely different doctrine which has nothing to do with the christian biblical doctrine of revelations, beyond using aspects of the name. Basically, all organizations and religions have a beginning and an end. The christians foresaw their own end that was inevitable and put a name to the Satanic Anti-christ Leader which will ultimately crush them! We put no belief into the christian belief, but if they wish to call my Magickal Powers and the powers of our Anti-christ Soldiers the power of Satan or their Devil, so be it.

So, there is no Satan or Devil, but there are many Antichrists and I am their Satanic Leader! I am a Magickal Antichrist! We transform energy forces and talismans to power we can use on a daily basis and to achieve our goals. We are currently trapped in a capitalist system which makes us all poverty slaves and forces us to use their money to survive. Our goal is to actually break free of the capitalist system, move beyond using their money, and be freed from the class system altogether. We believe in fighting fire with fire! We will use their money to amass the fortune needed to break free! Now, I've tried offering free methods and I still offer work alternatives for those who have very little money. Everyone who supports our beliefs and goals must join us and do their part by helping to support our temple and people financially or through work. Many people have abused the free member path and free title path. I've given these potential recruits hours of training and some up to a few years, only for them to decide it was not something they believed in or they became bored. Our time, knowledge, and effort is all very valuable and it's become my Church and Temple Law to make sure our time and energy is not wasted on these people who would drain us without thought or care! I believe I've made this reason for Member Fees absolutely clear!

Priest and Priestess Benefits

The Priest and Priestess will have many benefits. First they will pay their Lifetime Membership Fee of $100 and Annual Priest or Priestess Fee of $100. The Priest or Priestess will choose the path of the Warrior-Priest or the Holy Whore Priestess. Then the Priest or Priestess will receive their Basic Training and be Tested. After training and testing the Priest and Priestess will have the opportunity to run their own Group or Circle Sub-Temple and recruit their own Members. They will receive 50% commission based upon Member Fees. The job of the Priest or Priestess will be to teach the Church and Temple doctrines, practice Church and Temple Rituals and Ceremonies, Train in many Arts on their own, Help Develop new Rituals or Ceremonies, Recruit New Members, etc. The Priest and Priestess will each receive their own Satanic Bible version featuring the Priest or Priestess on the cover, their Priest or Priestess Title, Short Bio., and possibly some photos inside. Each sale of these featured versions will bring to the Priest or Priestess $50. These Featured Satanic Bible Books will be listed on hundreds of web sites for sale. Those Priests and Priestesses that also become a Satanic Kali Model will receive $1,000. The Satanic Kali Model will be featured in New Adult Magazines which are in the process of development.

The Satanic State

Laveyans tried for a long time to maintain a monopoly on "Satanism" as an organized religion and the whole true Satanist thing is one method used in that process. They have inferior methods of recruitment (despite their claim not to recruit) which undermines their progress along with a lot of other organizational blunders. It all comes down to economics. There is no religion on Earth that has become a world religion without state financing! The likelihood of a majority judeo-christian society and state ever financing a Satanic Temple is less likely than jesus resurrecting! Therefore, we must bring the state to the Satanic Society. The people who support church and state separation are deluded because you can never truly separate them, only to a degree. This is because the core of every society is based upon a specific moral-value system which is born in the heart of a specific religion or set of religions. The Satanic State will manufacture its own financial base and arise with the power of an anti-christian or Satanic Moral-Value System which I've worked to re-construct from many ancient religions, values, and ways of life that were naturally anti-christian.

Vampir Alchemy

The Vampir in my system is an ancient mystical concept and symbolic being which our Priests and Priestesses strive to embrace and become within our Warrior-Priest Order. This has to do with Alchemy, Spiritual, and Physical Training which will lead the student toward a path of immortality. We are to become a New Race of Super-Beings. There were once 4 races based upon ancient mythological beliefs. The first 2 races were immortal but the second one was inferior to the first in several ways, the 3rd race was semi-immortal or demigods and we are the 4th race of mortals. This was a result of breeding down with inferior mortal races. There are many secrets in this world and many people among the rich class and so-called royalty hold hidden keys to immortality. There are 2 sides to Alchemy and both lead to union and communion with the gods/goddesses and in my system the main deity is Satanic Kali. All other deities come forth from her as she is the Supreme Brahman. There is not a fear of death, but the idea of a Vampir in the aspect of a corpse existing beyond the death itself, is a mystical magickal symbolic concept which goes deep in the human psyche and represents our longing for life beyond death, and so an ever continuance of life, immortality! The christian belief of the dead rising from the grave at judgment day has also inspired the fantastic zombie apocalypse genre which is just more Vampir symbolism. It's biological warfare with mutant cancer cells that refuse to ever die! Anyhow, I have a much deeper symbolic system with Vampirs and it's an entire path one can take in my Church. As they say in the mythological jewish scripture, The Blood is The Life and The Life is Forever! I don't often quote jewish scriptures but most of their knowledge, beliefs, and culture were taken from more ancient and Superior Civilizations!

Spiritual Satanic War

We don't discriminate here based upon race or tribe, but we have specific cultural, religious, and political goals. Therefore, we welcome in our Satanic Temple everyone except those we ban. We ban the hiphop/rap subculture, christians, judaists, muslims, and those who actually believe in capitalism, the rich class, and money itself! Here we believe in a New Age Socialist System which will eliminate the class system within our Satanic Temple, eliminate money, and eliminate poverty slavery! As for the rest of the world, they can live any damn way they wish, but the world will not enslave our Satanic People. The world will not force a class system on our Satanic People. The world will not force our Satanic People to use their money. The world will not force our Satanic People to support their judeo-christian moral-value system. The world will not force our Satanic People to support their religious-political or military system! This is a self-imposed separation and those who will join me, will join me of your own free will! I ask you my Satanic People to swear allegiance to our Nation, our Satanic Temple, and to myself your High Priest Caesar 999! I ask you to denounce all allegiance to any other nation or temple and to join us today in the Spiritual Satanic War!

The Paths of the Spiritual Satanist 999

So, we have to look for better Women, who are more worthy spiritually to become our Holy Whore Priestesses because it seems we are burdened with nothing but the unspiritual type of Satanic Women here who are selfish and egotistical scum! They think they deserve to be a High Priestess when they should be crawling at my feet! If this is the type of Satanic Woman you are, know that you are unworthy shit! The Satanic Women worthy to enter my Temples are those who believe in the good of the whole over the self, surrender the ego, have promiscuous sex for free without money, and realize that your body does not belong to you, but to your people. You do not choose who you get to have sex with. You do not get to pick just the hot guys you want. You do not get to pick the guys with the money. You sacrifice for your people, your temple, and your god/goddess! In my temples the main deity is our Satanic Kali. We are a Nature Sex Cult with Holy Whore Priestesses and a Cult of the Sacred Martial Arts with Warrior-Priests! These are the paths of the Spiritual Satanist 999.

The New Age Socialist and the 15 Year War against Poverty Slavery

I'm disgusted by the state of poverty and homelessness in the u.s. We know that this is the result of the rich class and they are ultimately the enemy of the majority of people! There is no way for them to lie or try to talk their way out of the complete blame for the massive poverty slavery created by capitalism and the rich class creators of the system itself. We have come to the final state of reality that the rich class can not escape from and this is the final end for them as a ruling power on earth! The rich believe they are the high and mighty, believe they are some royalty, some special elite of civilization, but they are nothing but the scum of the earth and they will kneel before the world and return the wealth and resources to the majority of the people! This is it and these are the final days! No city under the earth will save you and no amount of money will keep the New Age Socialist from rising up in the final battle! The u.s. was already overburdened and its social services system unable to help the majority of u.s. citizens in need of food, shelter, and work. So, as usual the rich class and their corporations encouraged more people to illegally immigrate into the u.s. to keep wages down and avoid paying benefits which saves them billions of dollars. At the same time half of the other rich class owned corporations were given legal power to lay off thousands of employees and move overseas to make products cheaper and pay cheaper wages again. They also busted up the true unions and relocated their corporate factories in unorganized union areas. So, now the heads of governments want to legalize the 10 million illegal immigrants which have completely busted the social services system and have left little to nothing for actual citizens born here. They need a 100 billion dollars to boost social services and create housing, supply food, and create jobs for all these people! It's futile to keep complaining about the illegal immigrants but it is important to know the real reasons behind it. So, as a result we have to move beyond trying to push them out and just forget about that and focus on how the rich class government plans to house, feed, and give jobs to not only the illegal immigrants, but also the millions of citizens born here who are being led by leaders that have sold them out for political and corporate benefits. They pay off the banks and housing markets, and everyone else who ultimately directly affects their own pockets but where is the money for the people, the millions of poverty slaves? All through history nothing has changed. Look at each capitalist civilization and they have the same rich class hoarding the resources and keeping millions in poverty slavery suffering all their lives. As I said, the final war is coming and the rich class has no where to hide! So, the New Age Socialist must rise and wage the 15 Year War against Poverty Slavery!

Temple of Satanic Kali Dress Code

You may be able to now wear pants in Paris, but all Women will wear a Sari, Lehenga + Choli or topless, and or a Salwar, in my Temple of Satanic Kali!

Men of my Temple of Satanic Kali must wear Pajamas, Men's Kurtas, Achkan/Sherwani, and or Dhoti, etc. Dress style depends upon the status and position of the Men and the type of ceremony or occasion.

Capitalism Must Die

Poverty will not end until capitalism ends and the final defeat of the rich class and their supporters! The world can feed and house a trillion people but this can never happen in a capitalist controlled world. This is because the rich class and their corporations own and control the resources. The resources of the world belong to the people collectively and not to the rich few or their corporations. Therefore, we must ultimately take back these resources from the rich class enemy of the people! The rich class creates poverty slavery by establishing a system that maintains perpetual monetary separation and blockades. The majority of people are therefore born into poverty slavery through a monetary system that creates class segregation and grants total power to those who horde the resources of the world. The rich class protect themselves with laws designed to give them the liberty to establish and maintain such a system perpetually and therefore is the establishment of perpetual poverty slavery. All attempts by the rich class to end the poverty slavery is always a smokescreen and lies. So, do not believe anything they say and do not support any laws that protect them and give them perpetual control over the resources of the world. The corporations must die! The capitalist governments must die! The money must die! The banks must die! The rich class way of life must die! The land belongs to the people as whole. The resources of the world belong to the people as a whole. The essential step in defeating capitalism is to awaken to this truth, spread this truth each day, and never forget this truth for one moment! Capitalism must die!

Kali Worship and Meditation

I am one with Shakti. I am one with Kali. Shakti and Kali are one! I am one with Shiva. Kali creates Shiva from herself. Kali and Shiva are one. Kali is the Dark Mother of Creation and Destruction. Kali is the master of my mind! Kali is the master of my body! I serve and do work for Kali and she fulfills all of my desires. Kali's work is to build a Tantric Kingdom and Tantric Society. It is my work to build a Tantric Kingdom and Tantric society.

Kali is the master of my mind! Kali is the master of my body! I am the master of my mind. I am the master of my body. Kali's body is perfect, clean, and beautiful. Kali makes my body perfect, clean and beautiful. I make my body perfect, clean, and beautiful. Kali exercises, eats healthy, and trains for warfare. I exercise, eat healthy, and train for warfare. Kali radiates peaceful beauty when balance is maintained and war horror when the balance is broken. Kali consumes the sacred body that has completed its purpose upon death in her fires and escorts the eternal being into the new body.

Kali is the master of my mind! Kali is the master of my body!
Kali is the master of my mind! Kali is the master of my body!
Kali is the master of my mind! Kali is the master of my body!

Burning Away the Chaff

I thought I would let you know, that my temple is not all about the money. I offer work alternatives for those with little money, but most who come online surely can afford it, especially when they can afford lots of toys and gadgets. The purpose of Membership is a step in the process of showing one's allegiance and loyalty to my temples, my beliefs, goals, and to me. Also, they show a commitment to building my temple and spreading the beliefs. Lifetime Members can become a Priest or Priestess and earn some extra income, be popularized through my/Caesar's Satanic Bible Project by being featured on the cover of a new version which they'll also earn 50% of sales, etc. Finally, Member Fees and work will separate the seed from the chaff! The deceivers, users, and abusers will be sifted out systematically through this process. I've offered free memberships and programs over the years and most of the time wasted a lot of my own energy and time in the process. Most of those who receive things for free do not appreciate any value in such physical and mental contributions. They symbolize the foul rotten dung heap of corpses which we shall continue to burn and pave over to build my TRUE shining city of Babylon! I still await my High Priestess Holy Whore of Babylon and the prophesized billionaire to rise hand in hand for I am the High Priest Prince Beast 999. The Holy Union and Divine Marriage will build our Temple Nation of Babylon and a New World Religion will rise on Earth! Symbolically, we'll grind the bones of jews, christians, and muslims into dust!

More on the Holy Whore Concept

The Holy Whore Concept is a very ancient concept which can be found around the world in most pre-judeo-christian religions! I specifically focus upon the Tantric Devadasi System of India and work to restore this system within my Temple of satanic Kali which is the more spiritual temple I work on when compared to my main original temple/church Church of The Antichrist 999, which is more of a symbolic name anyway. So, the real temple that is rising up through that symbolism ultimately is my Temple of Satanic Kali. The core of my belief system is based upon a naturally anti-christian moral-value system or the Satanic Moral-Value System. This system reveals the sacredness and beauty of Whoredom among many other ancient values and ways of life that were and are naturally anti-judeo-christian and with a foundational belief which teaches us that a war of opposing moral-value systems has been ongoing since ancient times! Also, to briefly give you an idea of the awakening that I teach, you can imagine a judeo-christian priest telling and preaching to people that they are immoral or amoral for practicing specific lifestyles and activities and for a long time most people would just either accept that as truth and repent or revel and take pleasure in the knowledge that they are supposedly doing something wrong. And then I awaken them and enlighten them with a new reality! These judeo-christian priests are trying to maintain a monopoly on the so-called moral-value system along with their false god by teaching that their moral-value system and god is the only truth and this is simply their dogma! We truly hold our own opposing moral-values, moral truths, and ways of life that are just as moral, respectable, and honorable as their beliefs! We must never again allow them to employ such dogma against us! What I'm developing is a truly spiritual religion and not just a philosophy or what I call anti-religions like most of the other satanic groups out there. Our truth is for those who accept it and our reality is for those who enjoy it! So, when I say Holy, I mean exactly how it sounds as truly Holy, Sacred, and Divine! Also, I focus upon Kali Worship from the Shakti and Tantric Devotional Paths. Also, we accept a pantheon of deities but mostly as aspects of Kali since she symbolizes the Supreme Brahman! For example Kali symbolizes the entire Universe or Universal Consciousness. She divides herself to create her masculine side or Shiva and they unite in the Divine Marriage, from which all of the material universe is born into existence. This is part of the Tantric Creation story, which establishes all forms of Sexuality as sacred and divine from the very beginning. Also, establishes sexuality and sexual fulfillment as the ultimate form of worship!

Honor the Holy Whore

So, there are several orders in my temple and the two main orders are the Holy Whore Priestesses and the Warrior-Priests. The Holy Whore Priestess was worshiped in many ancient temples and also was the center of the economy in those regions. The judeo-christian scum have tried to cast her down from her sacred position and denigrate her by turning whoredom and prostitution into something degrading, disrespectful, dishonorable, and undignified. They tried to replace her with their false christ, but we will raise her up again, beautiful, respected, honored, dignified, and glorified! So, one of the many rights we highly support is our right to prostitute ourselves and pander. However, we recognize a difference between our Holy Whoredom and basic Prostitution which is for exchange only and personal gain and doesn't involve any form of spirituality. We prefer to teach and spread the arts of the Holy Whore which involve the more spiritual aspects and not directly charging for sex. The Holy Whore Priestess fulfills the desires of our Members and in return the Members donate to the Temples! The Warrior-Priests train in Martial Arts and defend the People and the Temples! All orders also train in church/temple beliefs, goals, spirituality, religions, magick arts, healing arts, dancing, herbs, massage, yoga, tantra, meditation, courtesan, etc. So, depending upon the arts and their chosen order, they will teach others and recruit others into their orders. We oppose highly overpriced prostitutes because the millions of poverty slaves can not afford their services which are reserved for the rich which we also oppose! Our bodies do not belong to us, they belong to our People, our Temple, and our Goddess/God, Kali/Shiva. Jai Kali Ma! Praise Dark Mother!

Tantric Hinduism

Also, I was into the cutting, blood, rituals, and satanic vampire type stuff when I was a teenager and have long since grown out of those practices. However, Blood and Vampire symbolism is still very important and ties into my arts of Spiritual Alchemy and Satanic Sorcery. The first term that must be understood is Satanic. In my system it's come to symbolize an Adversarial Nature, because Creation is naturally adversarial or is its own adversary! This is all it means and has nothing to do with a belief in the christian devil or Satan. I have evolved spiritually away from those more simple beliefs over many years. When I was a teenager, I was a basic devil worshiper, with little knowledge on the subject or experience. Then later on I was introduced to Laveyan Satanism and we mixed that with devil worship for a long time and then I became totally atheistic Laveyan for many years and have evolved beyond that as well back to a form of Theistic Beliefs, my own form of Theistic Spiritual Satanism. I find the term Satanism to be misleading or confusing to many and I have been distancing myself from that form of terminology, but I guess I'll always be linked to it. So, it makes sense to clarify a difference between being Satanic and being a Satanist which is where the confusion begins. The new terminology which I've been using simultaneously with the Satanic terminology is that of Tantric Hinduism or Tantracism. It's really the same beliefs, but carries more of the spiritual depth and is far less confusing to those seeking true spirituality and tantric beliefs.

Freedom is Finally Seen

What I teach is interdependence as opposed to total independence. My temple will be completely communal! So, the focus is to work toward that communal type system. People do not work for themselves in my system, they work for their Temple, their Community, their People, and their Goddess, etc. So, we work for our Brother and Sisters as opposed to the Self! To work for the self alone, is extremely mercenary and the base of the capitalist system which we highly oppose! So, the focus is not upon an exchange of work for money, it's an exchange of work for spiritual fulfillment and physical fulfillment just happens to be part of that as well. Here we sacrifice the Self, and the Ego! The self is secondary to the whole community! However, those who work for their people, temple, and their selves last should be rewarded with spiritual and material benefits of our Temple. All should be equally rewarded no matter their position or training and this is the egalitarian aspect. So, the idea is not to focus upon monetary rewards, since we oppose a monetary system, oppose a class system, and oppose capitalism in general! However, we will offer financial incentives during the beginning stages of our development, since we are forced to live and operate within the capitalist system and people have needs and bills to be paid through that system. We will work within that system until we can achieve our goal of breaking free from that system completely! So, this should give you an idea of the kind of people we do not allow to enter into my temple and the kind of people that we want to join us. When we own and control our own land, there is no rent. When we grow our own food, there is no need to buy food. When we make our own clothes, there is no need to buy clothes. When we own and control our resources, there's no need to buy resources. When the eyes are opened, freedom is finally seen!

Spiritual Rebirth

We've lost our tribal roots. We've lost our customs and culture. We've lost our traditional spirituality and religion. We've lost our craft skills. We know where the blame can be placed and that is a combination of judeo-christian and rich class interests in this experimental melting pot society.

I believe the u.s. is a total failure because despite the smokescreen of equality each social, financial, religious, and tribal group has continued to develop their own interests and many have betrayed their own people in the process. This is because old customs and loyalties breakdown into a mercenary survival of the fittest scenario under the pressures and hardships of the capitalist system. This is exactly what the rich class founders intended to happen.

The founders were mostly rich class masonic christian protestants and so huge supporters of the jews. So, it was part of their plan from the beginning to build a masonic christian and jew capitalist system. Today, it's now mostly controlled by protestants and jews, some catholics, with a majority of the people currently blacks and Hispanics. The rich class corporations encouraged the recent illegal Mexican immigration. The truth is whites are now the minority in the u.s.!

Meanwhile, the jews have taken over the media, movie industries, television, banks, major store chains, lawyers, judges, politicians, land and housing markets, building thousands of houses and condos, building hundreds of jew schools, building hundreds of synagogues, etc., and plans for a massive population expansion!

What this all means is that traditional White control and White traditions in the west will be completely undermined and mostly have been undermined already. They use the so-called democratic system to sneak up by night and use equality as a shield for their own personal expansion and growth with a true and secret goal of world dominion based upon their religious beliefs of being the chosen people of their god! The reality is the jews are using the u.s. as a breeding ground to breed millions of jews!

So, in reality there are conspiracies within conspiracies going on and in one hand the youth are crippled and blinded by the surface beauty of equality, and in the other hand made lazy by tv, computer games, and dumbed down by educational erosion, social-economical, environmental, and racial conflicts in the schools, etc.

My purpose is to reveal the truth that this form of melting pot system has failed and only the stronger groups rise above based upon their own abilities, loyalties, financial status, religion, specific strength in numbers, etc. Let's keep the jew conspiracy in the back of

our minds for now because I just want you to be aware of that truth and not to focus on that for now. What I want to focus upon is our confusion because we've lost and have been robbed our tribal roots since many of us are mixed now in this melting pot.

We've lost and been robbed of our spiritual religious roots with christianity paved over top like a new road over the old. We've lost and been robbed of our cultures and customs through total collision with other cultures and customs and cultural manipulation from the rich class, etc. We've lost and been robbed of our craft skills because of the rich class and technology which is used to bring prosperity to those who control the technology and machines which they build to undermine the Craft Workers.

Since machines produce products more efficiently and can make far more quantity than the average Craft Worker, they can sell them at a cheaper price than the Craft Worker. The poverty slaves are trying to save every dollar they can to survive and so will buy the cheaper product. Ultimately, the Craft Worker goes out of business, is forced to take a wage job working for the rich corporations that use those machines and therefore after a generation those craft skills are forgotten and lost forever! And the generations following are now slaves to the corporations as well!

So, ultimately I want to have your attention and focus upon a new beginning. It's time to start all over and have a Spiritual Rebirth, a new tribal set of roots is being planted, and new foundational spiritual religious system developing out of the chaos and confusion! We must return to the primordial fires to purify ourselves for this Spiritual Rebirth. It's time to relearn our old craft skills, relearn our old spiritual religions, and relearn our tribal customs with an understanding that many of us are now mixed and the spiritual purification is just that and not a total physical purification beyond being healthy in general. We do not want to repeat the fanaticism of the past, but understand and support the Spiritual Rebirth that was so important, but has mostly been confused and forgotten.

Natural Psychedelics

We believe in using Natural Psychedelic Plants, and Fungi, etc. to help achieve altered states through which we can commune with our Deities or Creation and for Spiritual and Natural Healing. We must not allow governments to control our use of Natural Substances, Life Forms, etc., that naturally exist for us to use! Our Satanic Kali created these Natural Substances and Life Forms purposely for our Ceremonial Use, for other animals to consume, and to exist for their Natural Beauty growing in Nature and Farmed! However, we teach to use these Natural Substances and Life Forms, for mainly Church or Temple Ceremonial and Ritualistic Purposes and not for overuse for recreation.

Secret Initiation Ritual of Becoming a God or Goddess

This is part of the Secret Mystical Initiation for New Members joining the Church of The Antichrist 999 and Temple of Satanic Kali through which they become one with our Goddess Satanic Kali and so experience their own Godhood or Goddesshood. However, this is not about ego raising and it symbolizes surrendering the ego and the self. One must be humbled and experience the Sacred Self-Sacrifice, Purification, Communion with Satanic Kali, and Spiritual Rebirth! This is one of several rituals that may be used by the Priests and Priestesses to initiate our New Members. The male initiates head is shaven the night before hand, the female initiate may shave their head if they wish as well and then both take a fast. Then the ritual begins by the initiate entering the temple room in their Ceremonial Robe, under which they wear nothing. The room is filled with the smoke of frankincense, myrrh, hemp, etc. Indian Classical Music is playing, maybe some Indian Dancers are dancing, etc. The Creation Story is recited by the Priest or Priestess and the initiate repeats the initiation oath, given by the Priest or Priestess. Then the initiate disrobes as does the Priest or Priestess and the Ceremonial Wine is sipped, Ceremonial Food eaten, and they begin to embrace physically becoming one, entering the sexual tantric trance. This may be the young male initiate's first man with man sexual encounter or first woman with woman sexual encounter. If the initiates are the same sex as the Priest or Priestess, there should be no fear or opposition to such a beautiful sacred and secret mystical encounter.

The Devadasi Fulfills Desires

The Devadasi Priestess fulfills the desires of men and women if they wish. They do this in worship of the God Shiva and Goddess Kali or another Goddess which become Satanic Shiva and Satanic Kali in our system. The Men symbolize Shiva and the Women symbolize Kali. The whole act of Sexual Healing and Sexual Fulfillment is ritualized and deeply symbolic which follows and reenacts the Tantric Creation Story. The Devadasi Priestess and Priest also learn many Temple Arts and perform them during Temple Ceremonies and Gatherings. Many of these arts include Bharatanatyam and other Classical Indian Dances, Singing, Musical Instruments, Massage, Tantra, Yoga, Meditation, Sexual Healing, Divination, Sorcery, Natural and Herbal Healing, Ayurvedic Medicine, Siddha Medicine, Martial Arts, etc. We also add many other arts like Belly Dancing, etc. So, this is a New Age Devadasi Temple! The Women Devadasi have equal status as the Male Priests and are Priestesses. They may choose their own lovers but it is taught that they should not choose just on looks or money and should fulfill the desires of as many as possible in worship and healing! The Priestesses and Priests may receive gifts and the Temple accepts donations and gifts as well.

The Natural Moral-Value System

The christians, jews, and muslims are liars and deceivers. The beliefs they hold are twisted, fantastic, mythological, insane, perilous, and by themselves will bring an end to humankind. They believe they represent the only good, under the only true god of goodness and justice, and they will all do battle against what they claim to be evil and falsehood. This scenario will bring total annihilation to the world and humanity. They call their evil enemy anti-christ and Satan and focus on attacking everything they believe symbolizes this evil which opposes their moral-values and laws! This ultimately means our kind will be forced to battle them physically in the future for supremacy of the world or we will face oppression and extinction anyway. Do not waste your time or energy studying their mythological insanity which only perpetuates their ridiculous beliefs and goals. I say burn your judeo-christian bibles or use their paper to smoke up, but their toxic biblical poison is not worth the risk to your health. I've always opposed their imbecile beliefs and it is important for us to live and breathe fire, live as Satan himself or herself, live as an Anti-christ! I am Satan himself come here and I am also the Anti-christ 999 and so shall you be as I am now, when you join me in Sacred Darkness which is a light yet to be born! This is a guiding light that will soon burn bright before our armies! Joining my Temple is the ultimate mockery of their mythological vomit and the ultimate sign of your loyalty and allegiance. If you must research, go back to the Babylonians, Sumerians, Egyptians, etc., because there you'll find the real original stories and beliefs which were later edited down, twisted, eclectically sown together, and then combined with their own centuries of mythological inventions. So, be what they fear most but do not practice idiocy! So, know where to draw the line or you'll become an ignorant fool reveling in the mythology of christian evil. Become your own sacredness, your own divine and holy being. Worship your own deities in the name of your own good and just standards as I always do. I hold my own sacred, holy, good, just, and glorious religion, god, and moral-value system which naturally opposes the judeo-christian, islamic beliefs and values! Now, it is time for you to learn these naturally oppositional values which pre-date judeo-christian values and mythology! I present to you the Anti-christian or Satanic Moral-Value System. This is the value system of many of the Ancients and closer to Nature. Therefore, we can also call this the Natural Moral-Value System!

The World of the Devadasi Revised

There are many ideas and beliefs I want to convey. In this article I want to reveal some of the lingering right-hand path and right-wing conservative values that are still being inculcated today, even in the more liberal youth. This is also being carried on within left-hand path and left-wing liberal groups. I teach that anti-Promiscuity, anti-Whoredom, anti-Prostitution, anti-Polygamy, anti-Homosexuality, and several other values and lifestyles connected with specific sexual institutions and cultural developments are mainly associated with and have their origins in more right-hand path and right-wing conservative valued cultures and religions. This means that I am saying these value related practices and lifestyles are mainly condemned by judeo-christian dominated cultures and did not exist [the condemnations did not exist] as extensively before their existence [existence of judeo-christian beliefs and values or right-hand Asian values]. We are more concerned with the modern world than the ancient and we have been experiencing the inculcation of the judeo-christian moral-value system in the west for several thousand years now. This has also contaminated much of the world's cultures and religions making them more fanatical and conservative within their value systems. This has been especially true with Hinduism, etc. We have seen Hindus under the pressure of christians [and muslims] to become what they call more "civilized" and less degenerate in their values. The Erotic Sexually based civilizations of India and much of Asia were already in decline [because of other right-and path and patriarchal religions] with the rise and spread of islam, and then christianity became heavily entrenched in India and work to inculcate their values to this day. The war of opposing moral-value systems is very ancient along with the war between Matriarchal and Patriarchal religious systems which also effect political/economic structures. In many parts of the world different religions especially Matriarchal ones had sacred sexuality and the Holy Whoredom with its Priestesses. Men's desires were fulfilled when necessary and donations went into the Temples. The Priestesses lived with great honor, respect, wealth, and glory around the world! Where Patriarchal religions began to clash with Matriarchal ones wars would take place and where the Patriarchal systems prevailed the Matriarchal systems were merged together and so in many places like India the ancient Holy Whores continued on, but under Priestly Brahman dominion. They still carried on the old ways and lived very glorious and wealthy lives. This is not to say there was no negative exploitation, but this is to be expected on some level when you have a wealthy class dominating everything. When you believe in the Tantric Universal Creation and how the Goddess Kali manifested itself into 2 parts one becoming Kali and the other Shiva and they unite together in divine sexual union, as all of creation is born into existence, you begin to understand why sexuality and sexual fulfillment is beautiful and important. So, it becomes the duty of the Holy Whore Priestess to become Kali and take on her role and fulfill all the men she can who represent Shiva. This is done in absolute worship and devotion to Shiva and Kali, etc.! This is much like how many other cultures and deities were worshipped as well. Everyone takes care of everyone in the community, united by

the Temple and the Goddess and God of Creation which are ultimately one and Kali-Yellamma as the Supreme Brahman. This is a very Socialistic Communal lifestyle and all are rewarded and benefited. The Priestesses also learn many other arts and practices including traditional Indian Dance, Singing, and Musical Instruments, etc. The world of Devadasi existed in a mainstream society for hundreds of years spread across much of Asia! It lasted for centuries even after its decline. Only in the last 50 years has it begun to degrade into simple prostitution which we highly support by itself, but look with disdain upon the religious cultural disintegration of such a beautiful and ideal Satanic Culture as we would classify it. The fanatical right-wing Hindus with their new age agenda pushed on by right-wing christian feminists and priests who wish to transform the Indian values into their own have created laws which strip the Devadasi from the Temples and this has caused the direct loss of all the traditional skills they were taught for generations to survive. Now, the Brahman Priests managed to first have the traditional erotic dancing taught to their wives and daughters. This is basically a method of stealing arts from a group of people they classified as a much lower caste and were working to eliminate the caste altogether. They then stripped out much of the eroticism in the dancing making it more conservative, along with more conservative outfits which reveal hardly any body parts. Most ancient Indian women went topless as nudity and sexuality was not so looked down upon in those times. We are seeing the last remains of an ancient world built around what we would term as Satanic Eroticism from our rebellious awakening from judeo-christian fanaticism and cultural stagnation. There were similar worlds across the planet and they resonate with our modern ideals and values which I classify as anti-christian or Satanic. So, from our Satanic Moral-Value System we see the Devadasi Culture as a parallel to the modern Satanic Eroticism which we work to build as we undermine the judeo-christian moral-value system in the west. Now, I get to the heart of this discussion about modern values in the west. The western youth are still being inculcated with what I classify as a judeo-christian value that opposes sexual promiscuity. They purposely guard the secret of the ancient Holy Whore from the youth and so they have no idea of its true beauty and glory which was held on high in ancient times far above the pathetic christian christ. We work to cast down their putrid pure image of their christ and replace him with the Holy Whore once again! The great lover of many will be restored and glorified! Hail the Holy Whore! The young women today have already begun to walk down the road of the Holy Whore but still they are very selective in their sexual encounters. This is more of an ego issue, but it's still relevant. The western youth are also inculcated with a selfish mercenary philosophy which is the base of the capitalist system and helps the rich class maintain their diabolic power over the masses. The Devadasi and all Priest/esses that truly believe in their Deities of Creation and who are truly Spiritual know that surrendering their ego is necessary for true worship and devotion. Self-sacrifice is all important for community and the good of the whole people of the Temple. During the height of the Hippy counter-cultural movement Free Love was a powerful liberal movement but even their sexual activities were still far more selective than is necessary for the true Holy Whore Priestess or Devadasi to achieve their goal in worship and devotion. Therefore, we represent Free Love times 10 and the resurrection of the Holy Whore in a New Age Super Sexual Revolution! We promote promiscuity and the Holy Whore to the youth and our people! We wish for them to give their bodies to Kali/Shiva or what we call Satanic Creation and ultimately to all our people in divine

Satanic Eroticism! Join our symbolic Church of The Antichrist 999 and our Satanic Kali Temple of Kama and help us to completely undermine and overturn the judeo-christian moral-value system throughout the world! Deny the christian christ and hail the Holy Whore!

Mystical Tantric Priests and Priestesses

I am a Mystic Tantric Priest. I worship Shakti-Kali in the form I call Satanic Kali. She is the Supreme Brahman and is Androgynous. She is the Goddess of Tantra, Dance, Healing Arts, and Martial Arts. She is also known as the Dark Mother. Her secret name is Babylon and she is The Great Spiritual Holy Whore of Babylon. The High Priestess represents her physical aspect and so takes on the embodiment of The Holy Whore 999. The High Priest does as well, but also represents Shiva her consort and The Prince Beast 999. Babylon is the Glorious City Nation and Sacred Satanic Temple. Together they unite in the Divine Marriage and all Priests and Priestesses symbolize them as well. All of our people are to be fulfilled through Tantric Healing and this is your sacred task!

Satanic Religious Social Club

The Church of The Antichrist 999 is a Satanic Religious Social Club for people who are anti-christian by nature! We do not want people who believe in the good verses evil crap or the god verses devil/Satan nonsense. We do not want devil worshipers but at the same time we don't exactly want atheists either because we believe in Satanic Creation as a deity. The term Satanic does not mean a belief in Satan. My definition of Satanic means an Adversarial Nature toward judeo-christian beliefs and lifestyles. The term Antichrist 999 does not refer directly to the christian biblical Antichrist. All of those who define themselves under my definition of Satanic are Anti-christians by nature! So, we are all Antichrists and I am the Antichrist 999. We are all one with Satanic Creation. So, I invite all those who are truly Satanic in nature or Anti-christian to join my Church of The Antichrist 999.

The Rights of the Holy Whore Priestess and Priests

We have mostly achieved our goal of restoring Gay Rights, but strangely new age christians pushed support on a legal level. And it had to go all the way to the supreme court with fanatical right-wing judeo-christians fighting it all the way! This scum actually believes this is the united states of christianity and it's their duty to maintain the traditional judeo-christian moral-value system enforced through state and federal laws. This reveals the ancient war which I've been saying that we've been fighting for thousands of years. This is a war between people of opposing moral-value systems. I call our system the anti-christian or Satanic Moral-Value System. We have many more rights that we believe in and must fight for against our judeo-christian enemies. We will have a much harder time securing these rights with nearly no support from new age christians which are also our enemies! We will take these fights all the way to the supreme court as well and will continue to practice our rights, no matter what their beliefs or laws dictate to everyone! Some of these other rights we fight for include the growing, use, and sale of natural herbs and fungi like marijuana, peyote buds, magic mushrooms, and dozens more natural plants and fungi. Some other rights we fight for include pandering, prostitution, polygamy or polyandry, etc.! And restoring legal age of sexual consent to a closer age where nature intended humans to begin having sex! This is one of those new age christian values which christians did not hold hundreds of years ago. So, we are combating a mix of old and new age christian values and laws which strip away our rights! The ancient Holy Whore must be restored to her former glory. Hail the Holy Whore Priestess and Priest! There is a difference between true Holy Whoredom and Prostitution but there is a connection with ancient sexual healing arts and our right in a capitalist system to capitalize from our own bodies. So, we champion the fight for these rights and work to educate our people about the spirituality of the Holy Whore and the respect and honor that must be bestowed upon these Holy Whore Priestesses and Priests whether they charge or not. We encourage them not to charge our people who live in poverty slavery, but support their right to charge as they wish!

The Star Dreamer

I am The Star Dreamer. I live in a universe of dreams. I make the thunder. I make the rain. I make the mystical sun rays. I make the grass green. I make the flowers grow. I make the stars and fill them with life! Here you will join me. Here you will see eternal beauty. Here you will forget everything. Here you become purity. Here you will find ever lasting love in my naked embrace. Here you will be reborn and live forever!

Satanic Equality

I don't believe in unity between different Satanic Groups, because we have opposing beliefs, different goals, and there is a natural state of competition in the world/universe for all resources, including human recruits. The only Satanic Temple I support is my own and work solely for its advancement. However, if we come across similar groups with similar beliefs and goals, we may create an alliance with them. If you do not join my temple and support my beliefs, you ultimately are my enemy in this war! When you join me, I expect your full allegiance and loyalty as you will work solely for our family! This is the philosophy of the good of the whole over the self and the individual alone. As you see, we oppose the laveyan mercenary self-god path which works to advance the individual rather than the whole family or group as one. A group of mercenaries will turn on each other the first chance they get for self-gain and self-fulfillment. This does not mean that we oppose our own fulfillment, it just means that the idea is to work for the good of the whole family and we will all be rewarded and fulfilled equally!

Three Types of Satanic Religion

There are three types of Satanic Religion and they are all modern. There are no real Traditional Satanic Religions, only pseudo christian by day priestly sects which worshiped their own invented devil by night and cannot be classified as Satanic in the sense of pre-christian worship in a Satan or Devil, because such a deity or cult did not exist before the Common Era. The christian theologians took many pre-christian deities and cultural aspects and twisted them into their ideal Devil. These completely culturally separate religions now became wrapped into the christian mythology with many people clinging to the old ways. Rebellious groups which actually worshiped the christian devil were extremely rare and cannot be classified as pre-christian Traditional Satanic Religious groups. However, they can be classified as post-christian Traditional Satanic Religious groups. Some of these groups may even claim an unbroken religious lineage which is most likely a lie because it usually cannot be proven. The barbaric christians systematically wiped out every threat to their religious dominion they could uncover and to this day still work to undermine all other religious groups, especially Satanic Religions.

The first type of Satanic Religion is more of a Philosophy than a Religion, which is mainly atheistic or holds a belief in a Dark Force of Nature, and or with a strong belief in the Self-God with no higher deity or power. This type of Satanic Religion is anti-spiritual, anti-religious, anti-mystical, with a strong belief in a realistic outlook on life and existence as opposed to fantasy, idealism, and spirituality with its belief and worship in deities beyond the Self. This form of Satanic Religion believes in self-indulgence and Carnal Fulfillment with a very selfish, mercenary, capitalistic right-wing political view. One example of this type of Satanic Religion is called LaVeyan Satanism. Anton LaVey founded his system in the mid 1960's. This was one of the Satanic Philosophies that built upon several philosophers' beliefs such as Nietzsche, Rand, Redbeard, Hitler, and many others. So, very little was originally LaVey's own philosophy.

 The second type of Satanic Religion is considered Theistic with a strong belief and worship in the actual christianized Devil, Satan, and Lucifer, etc. This type of Satanic Religion is also known as Devil Worship. These Satanic groups also claim to be Traditional and sometimes Spiritual, but they are neither. Many combine aspects of Type One Satanic Religion with their Devil Worship. Some of these Type Two Satanic religions cling to the good verses evil scenario and revel in the so-called evil aspect or try to reverse the roles. As for the Modern Luciferians, they worship the christianized form of Lucifer, which has nothing to do with the true Traditional Cult of Lucifer, The Morning Star, or The Light Bringer, which the christians wiped out. All of these Type Two Satanic Religions fall short of true Spirituality as they cling to the capitalist, mercenary, Self-God aspects of Type One Satanic Religions along with their hypocritical worship of a so-called Satan or Devil. Also, Type Two Satanic Religions perpetuate a dualistic system and foundational belief in the existence of the judeo-christian god through their belief in the christianized Devil. This perpetuation of a dualistic system and giving credit to the existence of the judeo-christian god is the most detrimental aspect which helps to fog and delude young minds, when the ultimate goal should be focused

upon unhinging that foundational belief in the existence of the judeo-christian god in the first place.

The Third Type of Satanic Religion is Theistic as well, but more accurately described as Spiritual, with a focus upon building a truly Spiritual Satanic Religion. This Third Type of Satanic Religion begins with a new definition of Satanic. Satanic here does not imply a worship or belief in the christian Satan or Devil. Satanic means Naturally Adversarial, based upon what is referred to as Satanic Creation. Creation is its own Adversary. This is a concept of a Universal Consciousness and each of us is part of this Creation. This Third Type of Satanic Religion completely breaks away from the good verses evil dualistic aspect that the christians developed, so that we can truly begin a New Spiritual Religion free from the insanity and dogma of the judeo-christian ideals and moral-values! So, one of the foundational doctrines of this Spiritual Satanic Religion is that of the Anti-christian or Satanic Moral Value System. This Satanic Creation can be worshiped symbolically through almost any other deity except the judeo-christian god and their christianized invention of a Devil.

Since this Satanic Creation is seen as a Tantric Creation, based upon Tantric Creation Stories which involve the Mystical Divine Marriage and Sexual Union of a God and Goddess, with a focus upon a Shakti Tradition, the Goddess Kali and God Shiva are adopted and known as Satanic Kali and Satanic Shiva. The Shakti Tradition puts the Goddess above the God, as the God aspect ultimately comes from her. This is combined with the Left-Hand Tantric Tradition and ultimately becomes a New Age Mystical Satanic Nature Sex Cult. This Type Three Satanic Religious path has a Communal aspect to it, which puts it naturally in opposition to the other Satanic Religious Types. This Satanic Spiritual Religious path is considered more of the Middle Way, combining Spirituality and Carnality! There is a focus upon restoring the ancient concept of the Holy Whore and raising up a Priest/Priestess Order based upon these Tantric Principles, along with a Warrior-Priest Order. Type Three Satanic Religion openly rejects most feminists, since they reject such systems which teach Women to naturally embrace promiscuous sexuality and child bearing. These feminist Women are often found in Type One Satanic Religions and guys there are not able to embrace sexuality with mainly feminist selfish Women, unless they are hot or have a lot of money. So, just remember that guys!

Spiritual Satanism 999 was created by High Priest Caesar 999, which evolved over the years which may have caused some confusion. By 1999, the core doctrines of Spiritual Satanism 999 were complete and the underground Church of The Antichrist 999 was born! Later on, High Priest or Rev. Caesar 999 developed the more spiritual Temple of Satanic Kali, which embraces more of the Eastern Hindu Spirituality and will be spreading these Spiritual Satanic doctrines throughout India and the Far East. Rev. Caesar 999 released his third edition Satanic Bible in 2007 which contained some older doctrines. The updated and simplified version was published in 2012, titled as The Satanic Bible 2012. These books are meant to teach the basics of his doctrines and the student's spiritual mystical education will be completed through direct teaching from the High Priest himself or one of his Official Priests or Priestesses. Spiritual Satanism 999

breaks away from all other types of Satanic Religion and represents a truly Spiritual and Mystical Satanic Religion for all the new generations to come!

The Death of Monogamy

Women are still inculcated from birth with the judeo-christian moral-value and fantastic ideal of monogamy. So, by the time Women reach adulthood most are completely brainwashed into believing in that judeo-christian value, or doctrine, and lifestyle. It is the goal of our Church of The Antichrist 999 and Temple of Satanic Kali, to break this doctrine and restore our ancient anti-christian polygamous values!

The Holy Whore of Babylon Rises!

She is our goddess Satanic Kali and symbolically manifests as our High Priestess of the Church of The Antichrist 999 and Temple of Satanic Kali. All of our Priestesses represent her feminine Shakti universal force which also manifests the masculine Shiva force. She symbolizes the divine Tantric Sexual Energy of the Universe as does her masculine aspect. The High Priest Prince Beast 999 (High Priest Caesar 999) symbolizes the god Satanic Shiva energy force and through their Sexual Union or Divine Marriage all of the material Universe comes into existence. Together our job is to spread that Sexual Energy and Tantric Sexual Healing Arts throughout the world, and Divine Universe or Universal Consciousness. This follows the mystical spiritual aspects of Rev. Caesar 999's religion of Spiritual Satanism 999 or Tantric Hinduism. This system combines aspects of his Theistic-Spiritual Satanism (Satanic meaning Adversarial Nature, not belief or worship of the christian Satan.), Shaktism (Goddess Worship/Branch of Hinduism), Tantrism, Buddhism, etc.

The Great Work

You see in my belief system there is an ideal. First there is the worship of the goddess/god in the form of female Goddess Kali and this is Creation. We are all one with Creation. This makes us divine as well, lesser aspects of the greater deity. There is only one mind, one will, one goal. Then we work to serve this one mind, through surrendering the ego, self-sacrifice, and total loyalty and allegiance to Kali, High Priest and High Priestess, the Temple and Religion, and finally to all our People as One Family. No one else in the world matters.

The good of the whole, is greater than the good of the individual. This is a communal philosophy. So, we frown upon greed, selfishness, self-interests, capitalism, the class system, and the rich class. Money is not important for the individual, it is only important for the Temple to use as a tool to help us break free of the capitalist system and live without money. The idea is to fight fire with fire and only use capitalism as a tool to fight capitalism!

Every man and woman needs sexual fulfillment in order for them to be healthy mentally and physically and this has been determined to be the greatest motivator in society and greatest morale booster. Sex truly makes the world go round and is the secret motivation of everything. It is therefore the chosen fuel or power of the great High Priest and Messenger of the New Religion under the guidance of the Goddess Kali, and will be fulfilled by the great High Priestess and her work when she rises and accepts the Holy Doctrines and Holy Orders. We are one with the Goddess/God and our bodies are born of the Goddess/God to serve the Goddess/God and finally ourselves last. Each of us is sworn to do the Great Work and sacrifice our bodies and minds for the fulfillment of the Great Work.

A Woman has two original true purposes. Her first purpose is to become a Holy Whore and fulfill men and women with her pleasures. This is why the Goddess made her so beautiful. Her second purpose is to become the Sacred Mother and bare many children and raise them. All those who oppose these doctrines are our enemies!

We are not to be afraid of disease or death, etc. because we will all be reborn and return to this world to fulfill the Great Work as we use all knowledge, Science, Medicine, Spiritual Healing, and Spiritual Religion all to achieve Immortality in the physical body.

Every Citizen, Member must be fulfilled and in return they must do their job working toward the fulfillment of the Great Work. There will be no bills, no rent, no utility bills, no auto bills or insurance, no medical bills, etc. Money will not exist and we will create a system that allows our people to slowly step outside the capitalist system. This primitive capitalist system must and will be eventually completely eliminated as a more spiritually advanced system takes us into the future.

The Satanic Singularity

The Great Holy Day of the Satanic Singularity approaches. This will be the Holy Day that the first Billionaire donates his fortune toward the building of Satanic Temples around the world! This will be the Holy Day that a minority Satanic sub-culture begins its rise to mainstream society and its march towards a political majority in certain regions of the world. This will be our Holy Day of fornication and pleasure! This will be our Holy Day of Glory and Satanic Resurrection! For this Holy Day will give to us the Herald of the Antichrist to come!

The Devadasi Restoration Movement

The Devadasi Holy Whore Priestesses came under attack by right-hand path religious fanatic reformers who wanted to outlaw Erotic Dance and Holy Whore Sexual Arts. Laws were passed that made being a Devadasi or similar Temple Dancers illegal and forced them out of their Temples and into the streets across India. This stripped them of their ability to practice their traditional arts which helped to fund the Temples and brought to them many expensive gifts for their services. So, many of their arts were lost. In an even more insulting manner, the fanatical Brahmin priests of the upper caste had one of the main classical Indian Dances which the Devadasi practiced which is called Bharata Natyam or Sadir taught to their wives and daughters, claiming to save the art in this fashion. What they did was strip out the sexual erotic aspects and give them more conservative outfits covering up their bodies. There is a movement to completely restore the Traditional Devadasi Priestesses and their complete system of Holy Whore Erotic Arts, especially Temple Dance for both the Deities and Public Entertainment. Support The Devadasi Restoration Movement!

The Other Satanic Groups

The other Satanic Groups like Laveyans and devil worshipers consider their form of
Satanism to be the only true form of Satanism. These other Satanic Groups try to claim a
monopoly on what Satanism represents. We were around before a lot of these newer
groups including the newer Luciferan and devil worship groups which are our natural
enemies as well. So, we are searching for the newborn Satanic and anti-christian minded
or those who have yet to give their loyalties and allegiance to the other Satanic Groups.
We welcome the new and truly interested to come forth and learn our Satanic Religion of
Spiritual Satanism 999.

We work to resurrect the Holy Whore Concept which is our main form of Satanic Kali
worship. The chosen form of Kali we worship is called Satanic Kali and is the main deity
of our Church of The Antichrist 999 and Temple of Satanic Kali. Our belief system is
polytheistic and pantheistic. Polytheistic means we can worship more than one deity and
pantheistic means we see the Universe or Creation as the Cosmic Deity. Humans are part
of this Cosmic Deity as lesser gods and goddesses and yet we are always one. In our
system the Universe is a Universal Consciousness which can take on almost any form of
deity except for the judeo-christian and islamic abrahamic god which we deny and
oppose and must struggle against until the end of time.

So, all must understand that we represent a highly anti-christian, anti-judaist, and anti-
islamic system. Our Satanic Religion is not just another Satanic Belief System. Our
Satanic Religion is based upon naturally anti-christian, anti-judaist, and anti-muslim
values, society, and civilization. These other right-hand path religious groups are the
natural enemies of our beliefs in a war of opposing moral-value systems on a social,
economic, and political level. These other religious groups have been waging war against
our kind on every level of society and government. Our people are constantly under
attack and have had many of our rights stripped away by these fanatical right-hand path
religious groups. The oppression from these right-hand path religions has been going on
for several thousand years.

We represent a truly Satanic or Adversarial Religion and anti-christian system. Those
other Satanic Groups try calling us fake because we don't support their egocentric self-
god mentality. These other Satanic Groups are the ones who are truly fake because they
care about nothing but self-fulfillment, ego gratification, greed, selfishness, etc. and this
is nothing more than petty capitalist anti-spiritual thuggery. These other Satanic Groups
have no real higher spiritual or religious goals beyond their own mercenary goals. These
other Satanic Groups will always be our natural enemies because they work against all
forms of true organized religion and represent what we consider an anti-religion.

These other Satanic Groups are filled with teenagers that just want to party and listen to
metal music. These other Satanic Groups are nothing but competition and do not serve
their people in any capacity other than teaching them to become totally free willed gods,
totally independent economic work horses, and selfish mercenary soldiers. These
concepts are what these kids want to hear and so they can easily manipulate these kids

into giving them their money. What this truly equates to is an anti-spiritual egomaniac who has to slave harder in the capitalist system to attain the most possessions and services they possibly can all for themselves at the expense of all of their so-called brothers and sisters. We all know that not everyone can equally achieve this in a capitalist society and therefore many more will suffer while the few diabolic ones get ahead. This is what they call Satanic Religion based upon master and slave philosophy!

Groups of mercenaries will only think of themselves and put themselves before all others, including their temple and deity. These other Satanic Groups will collapse quickly because of this weak foundational structure and lack of spiritual devotion. A truly advanced and spiritual group will be far more organized and last far longer. Therefore, our enemies are not just judeo-christians. We must be aware and avoid these natural enemies who are loyal to other Satanic Groups. Our supporters must have complete loyalty and swear allegiance to our Priests, Priestesses, and our Church or Temple!

Sexual Creation and the Holy Whore Priestesses

The entire universe (Androgynous Deity of Universal Consciousness and Physical Reality) is a Sexual Creation and built upon the foundation of Sexual Energy Forces. This is reflected in the Tantric Creation Story which is very beautiful and spiritual. Therefore the highest role models of our society also reflect that Sexual Creation (Satanic/Tantric Kali/Shiva), Sexual Creation Story, and Sexual Energy Forces. These highest Role Models and Career Positions are that of the Holy Whore Priestesses and Priests. The other High Role Models are the Warrior-Priests and Priestesses. However, we emphasize a majority female Holy Whore Priestess Order and a majority male Warrior-Priest Order which symbolically reflects Traditional Roles in most Societies. The Holy Whore Priestess represents the duties of the Sexual Healer, Lover, Wife, Child Barer, Food Preparation, Gardening, Gathering, other Healing Arts, Temple Purification, etc. The Warrior-Priest represents the duties of the Warrior or Defender, Hunter or Farmer, Husband, Healing Arts, Builder, Worker, etc. It is the Priestesses Duty to fulfill the Priests every desire without question but within reason to keep the Priests healthy and happy so they can perform their job to the best of their ability. The Priestess serves her Goddess/God, Temple, and People by becoming an object of morale boosting and healing mentally and physically. This is her sacrifice for her People, Temple, and Goddess/God of Satanic Kali. All forms of sexuality become beautiful and sacred, including promiscuousness and homosexuality. We fully support our People's Rights to Prostitution and Pandering, but we would rather our Holy Whore Priestesses not charge their lovers. However, we encourage all those Priests, etc. who embrace our Holy Whore Priestesses and Priests to bring to them beautiful gifts to honor them.

Tantrism: The New Revolution

All psychiatrists and psychologists are quacks and their science false. When they first began, they used their psychological system to enforce their judeo-christian moral-value system. Then the drug industry grew around them and their goal shifted to profits. These industries combined, earn multibillions annually. The psychological system they believe in is not real science, it's based upon theories and that makes it a mystical system. The government sponsors them and along with the legal system, lawyers, judges, laws, they work to maintain a monopoly on this industry. Many other mental healing systems exist and they too can be considered mysticism. When one of these other systems became popular and began to grow and take away customers and profits from the government sponsored mainstream psychological system, these people asked the government to help them out and together they have been waging war against the system of Scientology! So, Scientology itself deserves another look for those seeking alternative mental healing systems. Now finally, another mental and physical healing system called Tantrism is rising up and they will declare war upon this system as well, but in the end we will completely force them to collapse. Our new age mystical left-hand path system of Tantrism is a mental and physical sexual healing system that incorporates other purely natural healing arts will completely replace their psychological system and other mainstream healing industries. So, let us combine our forces in the war for freedom to choose which mental and physical healing systems we want and to take away all power from these quacks and the government to force us to follow the system they choose. If we let the enemy take our rights and control what systems of healing we must follow, then we will all end up in cold dark prison cells, chained to torture chairs, and doped up on their quack drugs from birth to death, all so they can profit! Join the new revolution!

The Job of the Priests and Priestesses of Spiritual Satanism 999 (Tantric Hinduism, Satanic Hinduism, etc.)

1. The Satanic Priests and Priestesses must learn, practice, and teach the beliefs, doctrines, and goals of Spiritual Satanism 999.

2. The Satanic Priests and Priestesses must practice the main rituals and ceremonies, and help create new rituals and ceremonies of Spiritual Satanism 999.

3. The Satanic Priests and Priestesses must recruit new supporters into the great religion of Spiritual Satanism 999. Satanic Priests and Priestesses will earn Temple Credits and other financial benefits for their recruitment work!

Eliminating the Feminist Agenda in the Satanic Temple

Modern Women have been granted so-called equality with Men. This equality gives Women independent financial power and control over men through sex and relationships. This is achieved through Women not only having financial independence, but also through their personal will and choice of mates. Most Women will choose the hottest Men for sexual fulfillment and breeding. When it comes to relationships they will choose the sexiest Men who will submit to their will 100%. So, Women spread this feminist education on to other Women. They also lean heavily upon values that help give them control. This is seen with judeo-christian monogamous relationship and dating values, the concept of possession or ownership of the partner and condemning of what is known as cheating, etc. Men can free themselves of this control by Women completely through a Gay lifestyle which eliminates the need for sex with a Woman or a relationship with a Woman. They can also partially free themselves from control by Women by accepting a Bisexual lifestyle which in theory would reduce such control by half, but in reality usually eliminates that control by 100% because most Women still cling to judeo-christian anti-Gay values for the control it gives them over Men, rather than the lifestyle itself being offensive to them. The only way to level the playing field for Men to achieve sex itself is to return to simple barter for sexual fulfillment and never to enter a relationship with a Woman. If the Woman will not engage in barter for sexual fulfillment, do not associate with her because she wishes to control you and have power over you. This is the real reason why fanatical feminists cling to the judeo-christian value of opposition to prostitution, because it levels the playing field, if it truly is not an oppressive situation for either party. When it comes to deities and worship of a deity, make sure that your deity or Satanic God/Goddess has not been feminized, or that the Priestesses or Women, and even feminist guided (brain washed) Priests or Men have not taken control. You will know this through the type of sexual fulfillment your deity or Satanic God/Goddess offers to you, the demands or rules of worship, and ultimately if your sexual desires are being fulfilled. If your Satanic God/Goddess does not teach that all Women should give themselves to you freely and fulfill the desires of all Men in the name of worship of the Satanic God/Goddess and vice versa, then your Satanic God/Goddess has been hijacked by feminists who want to individualize and compartmentalize the sexual power and control through their personal sexual desires, needs, and a female dominated relationship. The way to level the field here and take the power back is for all the Men to unite and cast down such a feminist hierarchical system and restore the Satanic God/Goddess that teaches worship through sexual fulfillment of all Men and Women within the temple! This leads to true equality and undermines the feminist agenda in the Satanic Temple.

The High Priest Caesar 999

I am the High Priest Caesar 999 of my Church of The Antichrist 999 which is also called the Temple of Satanic Kali. I chose the name Caesar as part of my self-initiatory name for my Church/Temple. The 999 is symbolic of our Satanic Trinity which has a deeper spiritual doctrine taught to our Priests and Priestesses. I've spent 27 years in a self-initiatory state of development practicing meditation, spiritual alchemy, satanic sorcery, physical training or martial arts, sexual tantra or yoga, etc. I am far from perfect and have much to learn, since life is about constantly learning new things and developing further. I am a Mystical Shaman in union with my androgynous deity of Satanic Creation, which takes on different aspects and commonly as our Satanic Kali. Directed and chosen by Satanic Creation through the enlightenment of the communion or divine marriage, I've worked hard mentally and physically to become the leader of my temple and supporters to bring to you the Spiritual Evolution. I am a Warrior-Priest, which is a defender of the Church or Temple, and our People. I train physically and mentally for this sacred work. My supporters can join this order and also become Warrior-Priests. I am also a Holy Whore Priest who practices Sexual Tantra or Left-Hand Tantra and helps fulfill the sexual desires of our supporters. So, if you'd like some free sexual fulfillment I am here for you. I would never ask our Priests or Priestesses to do anything that I am not willing to do myself for our Satanic Creation, People and myself. Our supporters can join this order as well and become a Holy Whore Priest or Priestess. The Satanic Holy Sun has dawned. Let the enlightenment begin! I am the Satanic Holy Father and the Darkness is my Light!

New Age Socialism Brings Free 1000+ Year Long Lifespans

This is one method of many I know they are working on for transforming us into a state of permanent youthfulness or immortality. You see how they already are valuing a single drop of the hormone at $1000 just for production? They plan to use this for the rich class and I expect that price will go up much further. Also, the government may step in and make the science disappear as they often do to sciences that will improve the health or benefit of humanity but will bankrupt the most powerful corporations and cause a spiraling collapse of the corrupt capitalist system. They'll do anything to try and preserve their power and wealth. The solution to this is very simple. If we have the fountain of youth finally mastered or partly, and as usual money has become the problem for us all to benefit from it, then it is obvious that we must devalue the money down to nothing and cast down the capitalist system for a more spiritually and technologically advanced system and that is a New Age form of Socialism! So, join us now to bring free 1000+ year long lifespans to as many of the population as possible!

GMO Points of Interest, Corporate Love of Money over World Health, and Moni-santo's Genocidal Weapons

1. Point one, most of these media groups are making millions of dollars from moni-santo, etc., to promote their gmo's. So, they will go out of their way to try and build support for them and second they don't want to get sued.

2. This guy keeps going about the science and saying to help starving people, etc. The real issue is the money that moni-santo, etc. make from controlling both ends of this linked market as they make the pesticides, and the modified foods to resist the pesticides. And the fact that moni-santo has put hundreds of traditional seed sellers out of business and working to corner the market with patented (controlled) seeds and suing hundreds of others who they claim are using their seeds or selling them. So, what moni-santo is doing is trying to create a mega monopoly and control food around the world.

3. The seeds are blowing across the farm lands and contaminating all non-gmo crops and creating hybrids, giving moni-santo legal power to claim they are their seeds and shutdown hundreds of private independent farmers and seed sellers. The reality is moni-santo most likely dumped their seeds across the land to contaminate everything! We are waiting for the whistle blowers to bring us the evidence so we can crush moni-santo!

4. The real evidence is mounting that the current seeds they are forcing into the market do not do what they say they do. The seeds cause diseases like cancer, etc., have less vitamins or useless vitamins our bodies can not use, yield less crops, destroy the land and environment, etc.

5. The evidence exists that moni-santo actively lobbies and pays off media, politicians, etc., to cover up the real effects of the crops and seeds all for profit. So, when they talk about the science, they are full of shit. The seeds need to be tested for years and only used for emergencies! These companies however are not thoroughly testing their products and pushing them out into the market with massive promotion and publicity all for profit. Corporations are legally responsible to their stock holders to profit, not make sure a product is 100% healthy. We have government agencies that are paid off to approve products that do not kill us immediately, yet kill us slowly. The health risks are more important than the small if any benefits in the current gmo seeds and crops, and they are using us as guinea pigs so they can profit.

6. If it was all about the science then they wouldn't need patents on food which should and must be banned and the patents made void! We will achieve this eventually, just like technology belongs to the people and not locked up and controlled by corporations so they can profit and create poverty slavery. If it was about the science they would spend decades developing the seeds and not experiment on the people and our children. If they truly cared about our health, they would be completely for full labeling and disclosure of all ingredients. Then we can all make the choice if we want to purchase gmo foods or not, which is our true right! They fight labeling the gmo's because they do not want their profits affected and it is so obvious. Profit and control is their goal, not human health and

science for that purpose. Their goal is to use science to profit! This should be outlawed and eventually will be as corporations and the rich class will be eliminated in the near future.

7. Many of these people, corporations, politicians, military, media groups, etc., who are supporting these gmo companies all own stocks in moni-santo, etc. We have to do everything in our power to stop these corporations from profiting, sacrificing our health, and exploiting the people all so they can profit! They do not have the right to do these things and we must bring their world-wide oppression to an end.

8. If these corporations are developing the gmo sciences truly as a beneficial act for helping and saving humanity, then the scientists would do it for free, give the food away for free, and would not ever complain about labeling the products they create. They would be proud of their products and jump to label them and declare we are moni-santo and we created these gmo foods. Instead they are ashamed, fearful of the backlash from poisoning people with agent orange, committing genocide through biological and chemical weapons, and they are angered at losing profits which is their highest goal, not some humanitarian goal!

The Conspiracy to Control the World Food Industry

To sum up there is a huge conspiracy of governments, organizations, corporations, and individuals, all trying to control the world food market, etc., all for profit and population control, etc. I support genetic engineering for true science and advancement, but this work takes many many years to master, maybe even hundreds or a thousand years. However, these organizations are working together to force the people of the world into using these untested patented seeds for profit and control. They try to convince people in pre-industrial or semi-industrial nations that they need their crops, fertilizers, and pesticides and in connection with the world bank, etc., offer them massive loans since they do not obviously have the money to "buy" those so-called humanitarian necessities and therefore put the people and farmers into a state of perpetual debt. And then the world bank comes in and takes their property, etc., when the crops fail. Do not forget the crops are designed to yield less and not more, forcing the farmers to buy more seeds every year instead of using their own surplus to re-plant or sell. What we have here is a handful of people, about a few hundred all in control of these world organizations and corporations who are trying to carry on modern day imperialism and feudalism with the backing of rich class politicians, military officers, etc., who all own stocks in these corporations and sit on the boards of many of the same ones or did at one time. It's interesting that we as a majority people could easily take out these few hundred people who are in control of such powerful oppressive organizations. However, others like them would just move up and take their places as their culture and way of life runs deep. We know that the entire system they are built upon must be eradicated eventually and their cultural economic foundations will come tumbling down. We have a clear view of the enemy in the modern world. Here is a short list of the organizations they work behind and there are many more not listed.

rockefeller foundation, bill gates foundation, agra, gmo green revolution, syngenta ag, future harvest centers, cgiar or consultative group on international agricultural research, gcdt or global trust diversity trust, fao or united nations food and agriculture organization, bioversity international or the international plant genetic research institute, the world bank, rockefeller foundation's international rice research institute or irri, cimmyt or international maize and wheat improvement center, dupont-pioneer hi-bred, syngenta of basle switzerland, usaid, monsanto, dow chemicals, ford foundation, usda, fda, who, usnih or u.s. national institutes of health, etc.

The Holy Promiscuity

I realize that outside independent women prefer to interact with guys with a higher level of organization, independent self supporting, and complex social interaction with a circle of male friends. And that is far beyond my capabilities, desire or will, and the opposite of what I believe in. My ideal female is a Priestess of my temple with no other desire or need than to please the deity of my temple and the people of our temple sexually. Also, to learn and teach the beliefs, healing arts, etc. I do not want women ambitious for other careers, money, or independent lifestyles or outside our temple ways. There must never be monogamy or christian type family structures. The form of relationship will never be dictated by feminist women. The only form of relationship is outlined by the temple doctrines. The concept of dating or courting does not exist. Our females become Holy Whore Priestesses and Warrior-Priestesses and wear the temple uniforms or style of clothing made by our temple people. We surrender the ego and sacrifice many desires which will only lead us astray from the temple beliefs and goals. A woman's true purpose is to fulfill the sexual desires of our men and other women and to bare and raise the temple children when they want to do so. The children must never know their true parents as all are their parents and are responsible for them all. When the Holy Whore Priestess loves many, there will be no way to know the true father and it is forbidden to use science to determine this for the sake of anonymity. Those that do so will be banned from the temple. The Holy Whore Priestess tries to give her body freely to as many supporters of our temple as she possibly can. This is the Holy Promiscuity. This is a sacred path and the highest honor for the Holy Whore Priestess. There is no other career with a higher honor or respect and she must be glorified for this career. All that oppose this doctrine are our eternal enemies and all those who support this are sworn to teach these naturally anti-christian values, these Satanic Values to the youth and pass them on to the next generations. Ultimately, we will root out and eliminate the judeo-christian moral-value system and family structure. We will completely overturn the judeo-christian moral-value system within our Holy Temples and Holy Lands! The Satanic Moral-Value System of Spiritual Satanism 999 will prevail into the glorious Satanic Future!

Sexual Healing and the Satanic Trinity of 999

In my belief system, the foundation of everything is upon the masculine and feminine sexual energy forces of Creation through which everything manifests into existence. This gives us the belief that all forms of sexuality are sacred and combined with spiritual love. Anyhow, we believe and teach many forms of healing, especially sexual healing to fight all sorts of mental and physical sickness, including depression. We believe sexual fulfillment given freely with love is a powerful healing force that will help to heal the mind and body. And men symbolize the god and women the goddess. It becomes a great duty, a Great Work to restore and heal the symbolic god and goddess within us all. And the Divine Union or Divine Marriage of the God and Goddess energy forces of the Universe repeatedly reenacted in devotion is a sort of meditation upon the Satanic Trinity of my temple, the 999. The Satanic Trinity includes the 9 for man, 9 for woman, and 9 in the center for the god/goddess, and through their union they become one and therefore we awaken and are enlightened to our own godhood. And we rise up to a state of super human immortality!

A True and Present Satanic Power

This Church/Temple is not an atheist cult! This Church/Temple is not a devil worship or Satan worship cult! This Church/Temple is not a black metal cult! This Church/Temple is not a Luciferian cult! This Church/Temple is a Spiritually Satanic (Adversarial and Naturally Anti-christian) Nature Sex Cult and Shakti Satanic Kali Worship Cult!

We are about being a truly spiritual religion with laws and regulations. We are not some after school club for a bunch of black metal teenagers to pretend to worship Satan and hang out and party! We are not a bunch of selfish mercenaries, drowning in an egotistic pool of arrogance brought on by the foolish belief of being your own god above all others as we are lesser gods and goddesses united with the Satanic Creation as One Deity. We are not a bunch of imbeciles clinging to inverted christian views and giving credence to the existence of the imaginary christian god by believing in the existence of the imaginary devil of christian origin.

We do not buy the mercenary individual objectivist nonsense. We stand for interdependent religious, economic, political, and social advancement! We stand for total allegiance and loyalty to the Church/Temple and we reward all those who join us. We openly recruit, because it is truly the most advanced method of growing. We do not focus upon intellectual pursuits or realism. We represent Spiritual Mysticism. Therefore, most of our rituals and concepts are highly spiritual and mystical. We live in a Mystical Magickal world and we sometimes can control this illusion of reality through our Great Work. We focus upon our high ideal vision for our Satanic People and Community.

We oppose feminist organizations and those Women who wish to use their will to oppose their true duties which our temple has outlined and resurrected from ancient civilizations and forged into our Satanic Moral-Value System with many other values and lifestyles which existed long before the judeo-christian menace.

We bring forth this Magickal Weapon to be used to undermine our enemies and raise up the Holy Whore Priestess and Priest once again in the world. This is a sacred duty to become a Holy Whore Priestess for our People, Temple, and Androgynous God/Goddess of Satanic Creation, which we more commonly refer to as Satanic Kali.

Those who oppose the Holy Whoredom and giving your bodies to your People, the Church/Temple, and to our Kali/Shiva, are our enemies and you will be outcast! We ultimately destroy the christian family structure and raise up our naturally anti-christian or Satanic Family Structure. We tear down judeo-christian society and law step by step and rebuild it in our Satanic Image.

I am the chosen High Priest, as it is I who bring forth the Spiritual Knowledge through which we attain mastery. All these other Satanic groups only copy or imitate what I have been teaching long before them and they do it in a feeble and disorganized fashion. We will bring order to the chaos and show you all how it is truly done!

All those who oppose us and work against us are our enemies and will be cast down over time. The enemy knows who they are and my sharp voice will reach you from a thousand throws. There is no thing that can destroy the true Satanic Spirit! And you who seek to defend the Church/Temple will also become a Warrior-Priest by my side. Now, your training will begin!

Modern Independent Women verses Ancient Interdependent Women and Holy Whores

I don't like Modern Independent Women. I like the Women of the 60's that believed in free love and similar Women of ancient cultures. There is something wrong with Women today. They have no problems with sexuality, but the Whores are not giving it up for free to anyone? I don't understand it. They are so brainwashed to be afraid of disease or so self-absorbed that they only share their hedonism with the best of the best they can get.

I see this mindset as stemming from today's feminist leaders and an extension of Women shifting into more male roles as part of their career minded independent lifestyle. The right-hand path conservative religious Women are also adding this to their moral-value system. Many more liberal Women still cling to many of those right-hand conservative values when it comes to sexuality and relationship type. A lot of Satanic Women are of that liberal moral view yet clinging to some judeo-christian moral-values concerning sexuality, relationships, etc.

These Women either don't realize that they are clinging to judeo-christian values or they know but still cling to it out of some benefit or purpose. The benefit of a monogamous relationship might be the extra control over their Man and it's realistic in an independent mind set and capitalist system to keep their family structure to the minimum monogamous state, to limit children and mouths to feed through financial planning.

I don't want our people and Women having such careers, or having control over their Men, or doing any kind of financial planning, limiting children, fearing disease, etc. These things all undermine the beliefs and goals of my Church/Temple. I don't believe in outside careers that don't benefit my Church/Temple and our People in some way or form. We stand against the Modern Independent Women and they are not welcome into our Church or Temple.

Since I can not offer all the needs of life yet for Internal Members I have to allow External Members to live the lives they want, careers, etc., but they have to pay Member fees. The Internal Members just do their jobs with no fees, and don't have money, etc.

What we are building is much like the Hippy Communes or Ashrams of India. One of our goals is to completely eliminate the christian family structure or more commonly known as the nuclear family which is designed to benefit the rich class in a capitalist system by keeping each family structure small and the wealth distributed among them so that the burdens of capitalism are spread among them instead of eliminated through interdependent larger family structures.

These are the real reasons why the Big Brother governments attack Hippy Communes and off grid living, because it means true freedom and escape from the burdens of the corrupt and oppressive capitalist system and means freedom from Poverty Slavery! Yes, we believe and teach against capitalism and that they force billions of people into Poverty Slavery around the world!

Banned Symbols and Approved Symbols

Here is a short list of banned symbols and approved symbols in our Church of The Antichrist 999 and Temple of Satanic Kali.

1. The Laveyan inverted pentagram with hebrew letters. We ban the use of hebrew letters.

2. The fire and brimstone symbol that Lavey uses in his bible for publicity. This symbol is actually a historical christian symbol and we ban all christian symbols. If you already have it tattooed on your body that is fine.

3. The inverted cross. We are not reverse christianity, devil or Satan worshipers. Again, if you already have tattoos of this rebellious symbol, that is fine. We just don't want to see idiots wearing huge upside down crosses around their necks.

4. The so-called traditional Satanism symbol which I find annoying and oppositional to my beliefs. There is no such thing as traditional Satanism, it's all modern. Those who believe there is such a thing are idiots.

Approved Satanic Symbols

1. The Star of Satanic Creation which I created for my Church and Temple from a dream I had. It was this symbol that led me to researching Thelema and discovering that Crowley had created a similar symbol

The Greatest Enemies and the Satanic State

The pseudo state military religious regime known as israel is the greatest threat to the world and the greatest enemy of the Satanic People! All those people and parties that support them are also the enemies of the Satanic People!

I don't believe in voting, because I don't believe the politics will change enough to achieve the goals of my Satanic Nation. This is because the very people who designed their capitalist system designed it to always remain a system they the rich class can control. So, as a Separatist, I believe that is the only true way to break free from the poverty slavery they spread. However, I've also come to the conclusion that the left leaning democratic party is just another false front for the very same rich class and of course dominated by a christian zionist majority.

If I was to vote, I'd never vote for a jew or a christian. Also, I'd never vote for someone of the rich class! This literally eliminates almost all politicians. The system is designed by rich people who have built up regulations, fees, media events, etc., around financial blockades which ultimately make it a rich class game by design. Also, these people are taught to never use their own wealth directly and so rely heavily upon contributions from the other rich bastards, corporations, the public, etc.

I strongly believe now that the democratic party is equally as bad as the republican party. Those of you who do vote would be better off with a third party and getting out from under the dominion of the judeo-christian zionist rich class parties as I've come to truly believe these 2 parties ultimately represent!

Personally, I have no confidence in their political economic systems and do not believe any real change can be achieved from within their system. It just will go round and round in circles like the merry-go-round and you're all brainwashed by the music and the horses.

I believe the only real solution is separation and to build our own religious economic political state nation much like the vatican city and I am the High Priest of our Satanic Nation. This is the only true way that we can break free from poverty slavery, judeo-christian zionist oppression, and technological limitations!

I also do not believe in church and state separation because it can never truly be achieved on all levels. This is because the core of every religious system is based upon a specific moral-value system. The judaists, christians, and muslims all share a similar moral-value system which I classify as the judeo-christian moral-value system.

Through my religion of Spiritual Satanism 999, I teach a naturally oppositional moral-value system known as the anti-christian or Satanic Moral-Value System. Therefore, what I see going on since ancient times is a perpetual war of opposing moral-value

systems and these different groups build laws into their societies based upon specific moral-value systems stemming from the religious views of the majority people.

Therefore, religion and state can never be completely separated, only to a degree. I do not believe that different cultures or religions can be mixed together into a society without one group or the other dominating the other and violence and oppression will result. Ultimately, these people will become aware of this fact and separate into their own Nation State! Join me, and my Satanic State!

Living True

We shouldn't worry about what others think of us and live the kind of life we want, right? We should fulfill the desires and pleasures that we enjoy and pursue the interests that fascinate and motivate us. We should do these things even if it ruins our reputation and makes us lose friends, family, or even jobs. The truth is, it does not matter what those other people think or believe. If they can't handle it or accept it, then they are not true friends or true family.

I figured out that most guys would practice Gay sex for the pleasure, if they were not afraid of getting a bad reputation and people outcast them. They are so brainwashed by christian culture to hate and oppose Gay sex growing up that most only accept the heterosexual lifestyle.

The Women are also brainwashed into that crap and most will not have sex with Bisexual Men based upon that cultural programming they received growing up. The guys know that Women will not have sex with them after finding out such news which basically is ruining the "reputation" of that person based upon judeo-christian culture and beliefs which still are practiced in a lot of families that are no longer religious or go to church, etc.

So, in my opinion most guys would enjoy Gay sex like the ancient Greeks, Romans, etc., if not for the christian cultural programming. This is why it's so important to spread my anti-christian Satanic Moral-Value system to undermine the judeo-christian moral-value system and culture! We will quickly return to the Pagan Hedonistic values and beauty of the ancients. Men will freely embrace Gay sex without fear of their reputations being destroyed as will Women with other Women.

Gay, Bisexual, Men and Women represent the front of Satanic Advancement in a world and society still dominated by judeo-christian values and culture! Once again, this is why it is so important to spread the values and culture of my naturally anti-christian Satanic Moral-Value System. The Satanic Moral-Value System can be found within my book, The Satanic Bible 2012.

Temple of Satanic Kali and the Duties of Women

In our Temple of Satanic Kali, technology is banned. We eliminate the technology of the modern world to return to a purely natural state in mind/spirit and body. Women will have specific jobs as Priestesses. They will become Holy Whore Priestesses practicing Tantric Sexual arts to fulfill Men's desires, practice several types of classical Indian and Arabic dancing, other duties, etc. The dress code will be of special importance. A percentage of Priestesses must always be topless, and others can wear some tops, like lehenga and a choli, sari, or salwar, etc. The ancient Women often went topless and we will restore this practice which is actually a right of Women to do so. Modern laws are hypocritical allowing only Men to go topless in society. We will begin these practices within our Temples and territories!

Satanic Mysticism and the Shamanistic Path of Spiritual Satanism 999

Are you an ideal Priest, Priestess, or High Priestess for the Church of The Antichrist 999 and Temple of Satanic Kali? Have you studied The Satanic Bible by Rev. Caesar 999 or The Satanic Bible 2012? Have you read Satan's Sorcery Volume I? Have you read The Crystal Tower? These are foundational books for the religion of Spiritual Satanism 999, created by High Priest Caesar 999. This belief system is also known as Tantric Hinduism or Caesarean Satanism! Have you learned about the Holy Whore Priestess and Priest? Have you learned about the Warrior-Priests and Priestesses? These are the main two Priesthood Orders. Have you learned of our Satanic Deity? This Adversarial Satanic Creation takes the main form of Satanic Kali or The Dark Mother in our Church/Temple. This can also be recognized as Isis, etc. We support worship of many Gods and Goddesses, except the judeo-christian god which we deny and oppose. Have you learned of the naturally anti-christian Satanic Moral-Value System? Have you learned of the concept of 999 and the Satanic Trinity? Have you learned of Caesar's Satanic Sorcery and The Mystical Vampir?

War on the Rich Class

To end poverty, we have to wage a war on the rich class, not poverty! Poverty is the result of the rich class. Therefore, we must battle the cause, not the effect!

My Kind of Leader

I am the kind of Leader that I believe in. If others don't like me, then I am not their Leader. I am the Leader of my people and when they read my writings and listen to my songs or my speeches and they agree, then they will have found their Leader. I found them long ago, and I will find them again!

Satanic Kali Summons a High Priestess

I am the High Priest Caesar 999, the Mystical Shaman Anti-christ, Tantric-Sexual Healer, Warrior-Priest, and the Chosen Messenger of my Satanic Creation which takes on the form of Satanic Kali in my Church of The Antichrist 999 and Temple of Satanic Kali. Satanic Kali also has a masculine aspect of Shiva her consort which is understood by our students who learn the deeper spiritual and mystical doctrines. Satanic Kali sends her teachings and spiritual wisdom through me and she has summoned a High Priestess for me and our Church/Temple. She will also receive direct guidance from Satanic Kali, to unite with me, giving her body freely, and dedicating herself to our Church/Temple. She will be the first Dark Mother Holy Whore Priestess and we will then spread our energy and power throughout the world together. All new Priests and Priestesses will take their guidance from our teachings and from Satanic Kali herself!

The Crown of Satanic Glory

There's another meaning to this tattoo on my head. It's a Crown. It's a symbol of my Royal Power. I am a Prince and King of my people. I'm sworn to fight my enemies until the end of time, if I have to. No one can ever remove this Crown! This is the Crown of Satanic Glory.

The Judeo-Christian Terrorists

Let them kill all the christians in iraq, to hell with them. The xtians have no business there trying to convert them and spread like a filthy plague. The government has no business being there. However, since they are actually christian zionists running the government, they think it's their duty to try and defend them. Also, the government helped create Isis, so they can continue their imperialist agenda. It's all lies they spit out endlessly in the name of a judeo-christian empire that is doomed to failure! What about the real humanitarian crisis going on in Gaza? What are they doing about that? They are the ones committing the crime, by giving the jews the weapons in the first place! The truth is that israel is a terrorist state and hamas and Palestinians are freedom fighters. The jew christian mainstream media will only promote news in their own favor, for their agenda and pressure the government to continue their agenda. We live in a world of lies and deception! The government is the enemy of the anti-christian and the anti-jew. I have only one government and that is my own Satanic Government! So, what are we to do? We can voice our opinions and sit back and wait for the day when we can rise against all right-hand path religion! Many do not know the truth and live in darkness and see only the picture painted for them. Many of us have awakened to the true reality and it brings madness to the mind in a mad political religious world! Many know the truth and keep their silence out of fear from the judeo-christian thought police. Are you awake? Are you awake?

Natural Adults

Humans are natural adults by the time we are 13 and no one should have authority to declare what an adult is but we obviously need to defend our rights against those people who do! We need to restore legal adulthood to an age closer to what nature intended and to give a little room for mental maturity that age should be 15! The modern judeo-christian moral-value system must be overturned! The war against the judeo-christian is ancient and the anti-christian Satanic People will rise! So, yes we will have many gay orgies and heterosexual orgies and promote promiscuousness, prostitution, pandering, polygamy, and Holy Whoredom! All those who oppose these practices and our rights to practice them are enemies of the Satanic People of Spiritual Satanism 999.

Spiritual Satanism 999 and the Healing Arts

Spiritual Satanism 999 can also be called Caesarean Satanism or Tantric Hinduism / Satanic Hinduism. This belief system combines aspects of Caesar's personal Spiritual Satanic Beliefs, aspects of Shakti Hinduism with focus upon worship of a Goddess, Kali Worship in a new form called Satanic Kali, Left-Hand Path Tantrism which practices Tantric Yoga as a form of Sexual Healing, other Healing Arts, Herbal and Natural Medicine, Spirituality, Meditation, Massage, Yoga, Martial Arts for Health and Self-Defense, Devadasi Rebirth, Indian Classical Dance, Classical Indian Music, Indian Traditional Clothing, etc.

The Mother, Great Kali

There is only one race, one culture, the race and culture of The Mother, Great Kali. All humans come from the Mother. All gods come from the Mother. All Priests and Gurus, come from the Mother. All ideas, concepts, and beliefs, come from the Mother. Therefore, the imagined christian god comes from the Mother. The imagined jew god comes from the Mother. The imagined muslim allah or god comes from the Mother. Therefore, jesus comes from the Mother. Moses comes from the Mother. Mohammad comes from the Mother. Buddha comes from the Mother. Confucius comes from the Mother. They have been separated from her for so long, that they have the illusion of separation and the illusion of superior existence. Now, is the time to return to the beginning, and return to the Mother! All illusions will fade away and the Mother will return to all people! The Mother is not fanatical and does not oppose nature. The Mother is Fertile and Nurturing. The Mother brings Pleasure, Joy, Love, and Life! Death comes from the Mother, since the Mother brings Life. Death is the return to Life! Therefore, we must live Life to the best in Peace and Harmony. Then one day the Mother will hold back Death and Life will flourish even longer! We must not be filled with greed or anger, or it will consume us, the Mother will consume us in her fire! War brings her wrath and all will suffer. War is the Mother's Pain unleashed! The Mother will bring down all other gods, religions, nations, and kingdoms through peace and war. The egos of men will enrage her wrath and they will burn up the quickest. Then spirituality will spread from her and peace will return. We are to Love her and Devote ourselves to her Glory and she will Love and Devote herself to us and ending our suffering on Earth.

Basics of Satanic Kali Worship

Satanic Kali Ma is the Adversarial Dark Mother! She is the Supreme Brahman! To worship Kali completely, begin by creating an alter to Kali. A man will take a ritual bath, then shave his head in sacrifice and devote his life to Satanic Kali worship and the spread of her cult and religion. Many pujas will be performed. He may practice many temple arts from dancing, martial arts, musician, natural healing arts, meditation, massage, yoga, chanting, and especially tantra. A woman will take a ritual bath and devote her life to Satanic Kali worship and the spread of her cult and religion. She may learn many temple arts from classical dance, especially tantra, meditation, massage, yoga, chanting, etc. We worship Satanic Kali through worship of the physical body and spiritual body as one! The physical reality and spiritual reality as one! We wear traditional clothing while entering the temple and may do so while outside the temple! We bring flowers for the puja! Burn incense! When during the time of Tantra practice, we may disrobe to embrace the body. Also, it is allowed to remain topless in our public domain and temple domain, like the ancients. The Satanic Kali Priestess offers her body and dedicated as Kali's body and other goddesses, to those men who represent Kali's male half of Shiva. Shiva must be fulfilled and so shall every man. So, the woman becomes Satanic Kali and other goddesses, as a Holy Whore Priestess she uses tantra to fulfill their desires!

The Satanic Kali Bookstore

Welcome to The Satanic Kali Bookstore or George A. Hart Publishing Bookstore. I sell books from my publishing services, Satanic Kali Publishing and George A. Hart Publishing. This store is now the only official website to buy my books and products. Purchasing from other sites will soon no longer be available. Also, beware of pirated inferior quality printed books from other sites. Purchasing from my store directly benefits our Satanic Kali Temple and People!

Please make an account and take a look at my products. I publish books in many genres like Satanism, Spirituality, Occult, Magick, Sorcery, Shaktism, Tantrism, Kali Worship, Natural Healing Arts, Yoga, Meditation, Martial Arts, etc. If you have any questions or interest in my publishing services, then you can email me directly or use the contact form.

Sincerely,

Rev. Caesar 999

https://georgeahartpublishing.com

https://gh-publishing.com